D1111456

PRAISE FOR *WHAT IF LOVE IS THE POINT?*

"I loved watching Los and Lex on TV when I was growing up. Now that we are friends in real life, I can confidently say they are the real deal. They wholeheartedly follow Jesus and continue to learn and grow in their faith, while juggling three young kids and incredible careers. They are truly an inspiration to my young family! Within the pages of this book are honest and real reflections on learning about the love Jesus has for all of us and how that loves changes our lives, no matter who we are or what we have done. They live out these pages in their own lives beautifully."

—SADIE ROBERTSON HUFF, FOUNDER OF THE LIVE ORIGINAL MINISTRY AND BESTSELLING AUTHOR OF *WHO ARE YOU FOLLOWING?*

"Growing up in the spotlight is hard, but Carlos and Alexa have done it with style and grace. They leaned in and trusted Jesus as they found a way to juggle life in Hollywood with seeking truth. I know they're an inspiration to many other Christians in the entertainment business. So few of us find that balance, and I hope that Carlos and Alexa's story inspires others to live a bold faith as they find their place in the world."

—CANDACE CAMERON BURE, ACTRESS, PRODUCER, AND *NEW YORK TIMES* BESTSELLING AUTHOR

"This is more than a book. It's a story of freedom, hope, redemption, and love. I couldn't put it down! Both Los and Lex's words and stories bring life. Being in the public eye, I understand the struggles they faced (and continue to face), individually and as a couple. I recognize myself in a lot of the stories they share. *What If Love Is the Point?* helped me heal from life's wounds. It taught me that I'm not alone and I know this book will help so many others grow their faith and live out love. I didn't want it to end. This book was so refreshing."

—SAM ACHO, AUTHOR OF *LET THE WORLD SEE YOU*, ANALYST AT ESPN, AND NINE-YEAR NFL LINEBACKER

"Fans of *Spy Kids* and *Big Time Rush* will relish the real-life adventures of Alexa and Carlos, but *What If Love Is the Point?* is so much more than a celebrity love story. It's a reflection of the greatest story ever told, one where all our fears, insecurities, and unmet longings get swallowed up in Love's rich and satisfying embrace. Thank you, Los and Lex, for sharing your heart so vulnerably and inviting the rest of us to join you in pursuing the only thing that matters."

—JODIE BERNDT, BESTSELLING AUTHOR OF *PRAYING THE SCRIPTURES FOR YOUR CHILDREN*

"Carlos and Alexa talk about real life in this book—and I don't mean the glamorized, Hollywood version. They show us what it's like to struggle in relationships, be overwhelmed by a financial situation, and wrestle with the world's expectations—then show us how they choose to surrender to God in the small and the big things. They love God fiercely and His love is evident in their lives as He shapes them into becoming who they really are."

—SAZAN HENDRIX, LIFESTYLE AND BEAUTY INFLUENCER, FOUNDER OF S+S GOODS, AND HOST OF *THE GOOD LIFE WITH STEVIE & SAZAN* PODCAST

"Los and Lex have invited us into their lives in the most humble and captivating way, showing us the true nature of God, who is passionately pursuing us in every moment. I couldn't put this book down and was caught up in the combined stories of heartbreak and grace. To know Lex and Los is to love them, and you will leave loving them more than ever and, most importantly, knowing the love of God in the process."

—MICHAEL MCDONALD, DIRECTOR OF STRATEGIC RELATIONSHIPS FOR BIBLEPROJECT

"What a story! In these intense times we all need the refreshing reminder that God is at work, especially when we least expect it. Carlos and Alexa's story is fun, deep, and awe-inspiring. Their life, story, and words make me want to open my eyes wider to how God is working when I'm not looking. What a whimsical yet deep book!"

—SARA HAGERTY, BESTSELLING AUTHOR OF *ADORE, UNSEEN, AND EVERY BITTER THING IS SWEET*

WHAT IF
LOVE
IS THE POINT?

Living for Jesus in a Self-Consumed World

CARLOS AND ALEXA
PENAVEGA

WITH MARGOT STARBUCK

NELSON
BOOKS

An Imprint of Thomas Nelson

Published in Nashville, Tennessee, by Nelson Books, an imprint of Thomas Nelson. Nelson Books and Thomas Nelson are registered trademarks of HarperCollins Christian Publishing, Inc.

Published in association with The Bindery Agency, www.TheBinderyAgency.com.

Thomas Nelson titles may be purchased in bulk for educational, business, fund-raising, or sales promotional use. For information, please email SpecialMarkets@ThomasNelson. com.

Library of Congress Cataloging-in-Publication Data

Names: PenaVega, Alexa, 1988- author. | PenaVega, Carlos, 1989- author.
Title: What if love is the point?: living for Jesus in a self-consumed world / Alexa and
    Carlos PenaVega ; with Margot Starbuck.
Description: Nashville, Tennessee: Thomas Nelson, [2022] | Summary: "Popular actors
    Carlos and Alexa PenaVega share their inspiring stories of transformation, from
    feeling lost and searching for meaning to realizing that living for Jesus and loving
    others is what life is all about"-- Provided by publisher.
Identifiers: LCCN 2022001960 (print) | LCCN 2022001961 (ebook) | ISBN
    9781400234844 (hc) | ISBN 9781400234851 (ebook)
Subjects: LCSH: PenaVega, Alexa, 1988---Religion. | PenaVega, Carlos, 1989---Religion. |
    Television actors and actresses--United States--Biography.
Classification: LCC PN2285 .P46 2022 (print) | LCC PN2285 (ebook) | DDC
    791.4502/80922 [B]--dc23/eng/20220405
LC record available at https://lccn.loc.gov/2022001960
LC ebook record available at https://lccn.loc.gov/2022001961

Printed in the United States of America

22 23 24 25 26 LSC 10 9 8 7 6 5 4 3 2 1

To the two people who were instrumental in leading us to Jesus: Andrew Mortaza and Amy Joyce. Thank you for showing us what His love looks like through your unwavering reverence.

CONTENTS

PREFACE

If you're hungry for something more out of life, we get it. If you've been out there hustling and still haven't found the peace and satisfaction you thought you'd have by now, we feel you. We've been there.

We know what it feels like to be broken. Aimless. Yearning for more. When each of us was at our lowest, we found—we were found by!—the One who made us, knows us, and loves us. And as a result, today we experience the purpose we were after. The hope. The fulfillment. And that's why we're eager to share what that looks like for us today.

But come on, why the heck should you believe us?

Living in the limelight of Hollywood can appear pretty glamorous. And so we don't expect you to just take our word for it when we announce that Jesus changed our lives. (Fer real, what does that even *mean*?!) That's why we'd like to *show you* by sharing our journeys that brought us to the point of desperation and, ultimately, love. Because we've been loved by God and are purposing to love like He loved us, we continue to discover what we were made for.

If you've ever asked yourself "What's the point?" we hope you'll take this journey with us.

Lex and Los

CHAPTER 1

BIG TIME

LOS

I'll take Ginger Spice and you get Baby Spice."

As a twelve-year-old I thought the Spice Girls were pretty hot, and I'd picked my favorite one, generously allowing my best friend, Corbin, to choose any of the remaining ones. The Spice Girls movie had been out for a few years, and I was totally into them.

I also saw the movie *Spy Kids* that year—like everyone else I knew—but, frankly, I didn't care for it. I didn't like the looks of that girl who played Carmen. I think her name was *Alexa*? She was too tomboy for my tastes. No, I was still all about Ginger Spice.

The possibility of actually being *in* the entertainment business wasn't even a thought in my head as I started middle school. As a six-year-old I'd auditioned for the American Heritage honor boys choir, and my mom realized I could sing. Then in middle school, when I earned the coveted role of Edward the Bellboy in my school's equity production of *Titanic the Musical*, my mom discovered I could act. So when she saw an ad for a talent agency that sent kids on auditions for modeling and acting, she and I were all in.

The first gig I booked was like a dream come true for this boy:

a television commercial for Super Soaker water guns. *I get paid for running around shooting other kids with a water gun? Yes, please.* As I started booking other jobs, I fell in love with acting. And as awesome as it was for my younger brothers and friends to catch me on-screen in a commercial, a little seed of possibility had been planted in my heart. I wanted to be in a television show. But not just any television show; I wanted to be on the Disney Channel. During the breaks between shows, I'd watched my favorite actors trace invisible Mickey Mouse ears with a magic wand as they announced, "You're watching the Disney Channel!" I'd even practice drawing the ears in my bathroom. So I was ready.

When I was in sixth grade, my parents learned about a talent competition in Los Angeles, where young performers had the opportunity to be seen by people in the entertainment business. The entry fee was steep—in the thousands—but my parents believed in me and were willing to invest in my success. So my mom and I flew out to LA, while my dad stayed back in Florida with my three younger brothers and his job running a successful business of importing and exporting frozen Latin foods. On the weekend of the competition, one of the people in the audience turned out to be the casting director for Nickelodeon, and she took notice when the emcee of the event announced that I won "Best Male Actor." And "Best Male Model." And "Best Male in a Commercial." And "Best Overall Talent." Each time I heard this guy say "Carlos Pena," I knew I was one step closer to acting on television.

After securing an agent and manager, I got the opportunity to do a screen test and audition for a new Nickelodeon show called *Ned's Declassified School Survival Guide* about a seventh-grade kid and his survival tips to help students navigate the challenges of middle school. I was still riding the high of all the accolades from the talent competition, and because I felt like I'd done pretty well during the screen test, I was disappointed I wasn't chosen to be on the show. But two good things happened as a result of that audition. First, I'd been *seen*. I'd gotten my foot in the door at Nickelodeon. And second, but equally important, it was the moment my parents became convinced that I had something special. And they were all about it.

My dad and mom decided that I would stay in Los Angeles so that I could pursue an acting career. Leasing me an apartment in Park La Brea, hiring an *abuelita* (aka nanny-for-teenager), and renting us a car, my parents made it possible for me to continue to audition for roles. At fourteen I felt pretty grown up, but even I could admit that I wasn't ready to be on my own in LA. So besides homeschooling, my life was just prepping for and going on auditions. With the help of my manager and agent, I booked some things here and there—another commercial, a spot on *Judging Amy*, a spot on *ER*—and kept hustling.

It's no surprise that I was not the best manager of all that freedom. I started screwing up in school, and when my parents learned that my grades had tanked, I knew that I needed to be scared. Trust me when I say that my parents don't tolerate lax behavior. They lavished my brothers and me with privileges, gifts, and opportunities as we grew up, but they also expected us to be doing what we were supposed to be doing. And coming home with a C on a report card just didn't fly. Neither did the time my mom caught one of my brothers smoking. She almost paddled him to death with her sandal. Their expectations for us were high, and when we misbehaved, there were consequences.

On the phone call I dreaded but knew was coming, they let me know that it was over. They weren't paying money for me to goof off. They canceled the car, ended the lease (losing money on both), said goodbye to the abuelita, and bought me a one-way ticket back to Florida. I was bummed that I hadn't booked a show or made it big, but I'd always known that my parents didn't play. I'd blown my shot.

So I went back to living at home with my parents and three brothers, Antonio, Javi, and Andres, in Weston, Florida, focusing on musical theater while I attended my final three years of high school. During my sophomore year I got to audition for a rebrand of the 1970s Latino boy band Menudo, a reality series called *Making Menudo.* It was an amazing opportunity and seemed like a great fit. My mom is Dominican and my dad, who was born in Venezuela, is Spanish. We were a bilingual family at home: English for everyday, and Spanish when we were in trouble. The Menudo opportunity felt *so right.*

When I found out I was cut from the next round of auditions and didn't make the band, I was heartbroken. Anyone who knows me well will tell you that I have very big feels. I like to think it's a Latin thing. So when I didn't get the Menudo gig, I decided I was *so over everything.* Music? Done! Hollywood? Done! Maybe some musical theater, but that was it.

And then, during my senior year, the manager who'd signed me in LA called to see if I wanted to audition for a remake of the 1980 film *Fame* about students at the New York Academy of Performing Arts. *Okay, maybe I'm not totally over it.* But you see the irony, right? It's a movie about teenagers with big dreams to make it in the entertainment business as dancers, actors, musicians, and vocalists. The audience celebrates their triumphs and grieves their disappointments. And now I was being given another opportunity to be one of those performers who could celebrate a success. After sending in an audition tape, I was invited to fly to LA to meet with producers. Before I'd even flown back home to Florida, I learned that the producers had decided to pass on me.

What?! I am so over this mess! I'm really done this time!

I didn't need Hollywood. I'd earned a scholarship to the Boston Conservatory, where I planned to go to college to prepare for a career on Broadway. And when *Fame* was a dead end, I became more resolved than ever to prepare myself to build a professional life in New York after college graduation.

The day before my flight to return home to Florida, my manager, with whom I was staying, called me into his kitchen.

"Carlos," he began, "I got you an audition for a Nickelodeon show. It's about a boy band, and they've invited you to audition tomorrow."

"You're kidding, right?" I said.

"No, it's a great opportunity, and since you're in town—" he began.

"No way!" I barked. "Menudo messed me up, man. No way I'm doing a boy band. I'm going to be on Broadway."

"Carlos," he pleaded, "you're here. Let's just do it. We'll make a tape and deliver it to them today."

"Fine," I said, "but I'm not singing on the tape."

He eventually broke through my fiery wall of fury. And since I wasn't flying out until the following afternoon, we made a tape and sent it to the studio.

The next morning I was packing up my clothes when my manager popped into my room. Prepared for him to deliver more bad news, I braced myself for the worst.

"They want to see you this morning," he gushed.

"What?" I asked. "Who?"

"The Nickelodeon producers want to meet with you in the studio this morning," he repeated.

"Uhh . . ." I said, trying to organize my thoughts. "I'm supposed to fly out at one, but I'll see if my parents can change my flight."

"Great," he confirmed, "we'll leave in an hour."

"Okay," I agreed, feeling dazed.

I would go, I told myself, but I wouldn't get my hopes up.

The meeting at the studio went well. It was going to be a show about four hockey-playing best friends from Minnesota who are selected to form a boy band in Los Angeles. After the meeting, the producers wanted to have me back *again* the same week, so my parents rebooked the ticket a second time.

I stayed another week and a half to do more screen-testing before finally flying home.

While I thought the time in the studio had gone great, I knew not to pin my hopes on a role that was more than likely to end in disappointment.

I'd been home a week and was at the movie theater watching *Wall-E* with my brother Andres when an unknown number came up on my caller ID.

Answering the call, I whispered, "Hey, who's this?"

"You booked the show!"

"What?!" I yelled, louder than I should have.

Scrambling out of the theater, I hustled to the hallway to hear more. They told me they'd shoot the pilot in October and then we'd have to wait for who-knows-how-long to see if it would get picked up. Because I knew how these things went, I continued to live my life.

Sort of.

I started school at the Boston Conservatory in August and left to shoot the pilot two months later. When I say I "sort of" lived my life, I mean that I did go to classes and get a girlfriend, Cassie. But if I was going to have my own TV show, did I really need to write *all* the papers for my courses (you see a pattern)?

When months went by and Nickelodeon didn't call, I realized I needed to rethink my academic strategy. And when summer rolled around, we'd still not heard back. At the end of the summer, as I was preparing to return to school and give it more effort than I had my first year, my manager called to tell me that Nickelodeon had picked up the show for thirteen episodes and I'd need to move to LA by September.

I'd sworn I was done with Hollywood.

I'd thought I was done with boy bands.

But it seems I wasn't.

So much about this particular opportunity seemed to have my name on it. Okay, the role of Carlos Garcia literally had my name on it. I was born in Columbia, Missouri, and spent the first nine years of my life there, so the Midwestern Minnesotan I'd be playing wasn't a total stranger.

It's weird, right? I'd tried to be a part of *Making Menudo*, about a boy band. I'd tried to be in *Fame*, about kids struggling to make it in the business. And now I'd be starring in a show about a regular kid who *did* make it in LA, and around the world, as part of a boy band phenom.

And it was crazy that I'd only been in LA for that first audition because I'd been in town to get rejected for the role on *Fame*. I was fortunate to have been in the right place at the right time. Although I didn't have the spiritual eyes to see it at the time, I can see now that God had given me that amazing opportunity to star on the show *Big Time Rush*.

Rather than returning to college for my sophomore year, I moved to LA a second time at the age of nineteen. The show offered me a $7,500 relocation fee to move my life, so I got an apartment and leased a car with my dad's assistance. He even came out and helped me get set up. But although he was doing all these things to help me, he didn't show any emotion. The magnitude of what I was facing didn't seem to faze him. It was like a job for him. In and out. I needed more than help installing the big-screen TV and assembling the IKEA furniture. This was a huge step for me, and I wanted reassurance from him that I was doing the right thing. I wanted him to tell me that dropping out of college was okay and that he was proud of my decision to follow my dreams.

After I dropped him off at the airport to fly home, I remember pulling over into a fast-food parking lot and calling my mom.

"I don't want to do this," I confided in her. "I'm all alone now."

She talked me off the ledge, and I sucked it up. This was my big chance, and I was going to make the most of it.

When I showed up for my first day of work on a Monday morning, I was sent directly to hair and makeup. From the start I really liked my costars, Kendall, James, and Logan. Like me, they got to keep their real-life first names for the characters they played. Kendall was the leader of the group. James was the pretty boy. Logan was the smart one. And I was the zany, fun-loving guy. I won't speak for the others, but the Carlos Garcia character was a pretty good match for Carlos Pena, the real-life guy.

There we were: four teenage alpha males jockeying for screen time and who was going to sing lead on various parts of songs. When we received scripts we'd approach them by doing these calculations. We'd count our lines and get miffed if another guy had more. If I had ten, I wanted more. If Kendall had a hundred, he wanted more. We were a real treat for the writers. Today we all laugh about how we behaved, but I can't imagine it was fun for our producers.

I might listen to a song we got from the producer and go back to him and say, "I'm barely on this song. I'm not happy. Can you put me in more?"

Then, if he made the mistake of obliging me, one of the other guys would go back to him and complain, "You took away some of my parts."

Beginning on Mondays, we'd work sixty to seventy hours a week. Industry regulations required giving actors a twelve-hour turnaround between shoots, so if we worked until ten one night, we couldn't begin shooting until ten the next morning. So sometimes, if we couldn't start until one or two in the afternoon on Friday, the schedule could get pushed back so much we'd be working into the wee Saturday morning hours. We'd call these Fraturdays.

I had a great time with the guys on set, but because all of them already lived in LA, surrounded by family and friends, they all had their own lives outside of work. Not me. After work I'd drive into the parking garage of my building, shuttle up the elevator, and file into my apartment. Like a robot I'd move from one box, my Audi A5, into another box, the elevator, and into another box, my one-bedroom apartment. Although I was pumped to be living the dream in LA, I was feeling really lonely when I wasn't on set.

I was still dating Cassie, my girlfriend from college, but she was studying in Boston. We connected as often as we could on video calls, but there are a lot of miles between Los Angeles and Boston (2,983 if you were wondering). When I could, I'd get off work on Friday, drive straight to the airport, and fly out to see her for the weekend. Other weekends I might make the same quick turnaround trip to Florida to see my family. But on the weekends I wasn't traveling, I filled the void with endless video games, movie marathons, pizza Hot Pockets, and ice cream. Every night I'd alternate scoops of slow-churned Breyers chocolate chip cookie dough and mint chocolate chip. They became my faithful friends.

When the first season of the show was a hit, *Big Time Rush* was picked up for another season, and we announced our first tour as a band. That's when my weekends really picked up. We'd spend a whole week filming until late in the night, and then when we wrapped on Friday, we'd be flown on a red-eye to New York or some other state where we would have a show. Saturday morning we'd be ushered to a venue where we'd shower, change clothes, and do a sound check. We'd do the show Saturday night, hit the hotel, and Sunday we'd be flown back to Los Angeles to catch a few hours of sleep before being required to be back on the set first thing Monday morning.

Week after week we kept this schedule. Performing at Jones Beach in New Jersey, the Minnesota State Fair, and even an arena in Mexico City. And although the schedule was pretty brutal, I always enjoyed performing. Being onstage in front of an audience was where I felt most alive.

When we wrapped shooting a season, we'd tour during the summer months in an entourage of over fifteen trucks and buses. On a typical day we'd wake up on the tour bus, eat breakfast, work out, do a sound check, do a meet-and-greet, eat lunch, chill, and then start getting ready around five or six. During the day, the crew would have built the set we'd use at the venue. We'd be onstage by seven thirty—hey, our fans were *kids*—and be offstage by nine thirty. While we'd shower and clean up, the crew would break down the set and load it all back on the trucks. Then we'd drive all night to the next city. We'd do as many as seventy-five dates in one summer.

I mentioned that our fans were kids, but of course those kids have moms. And sometimes at our meet-and-greets, a dad might be taking a picture of us with his daughter and wife, and the mom would grab our butts! Truly, the other guys will confirm this. It happened more than you want to know.

In some ways, we were living the rock-star life during those summer months on tour. If one of the guys saw a girl he liked in the crowd, he could ask security to communicate with "the girl in the pink shirt in the second row." Then security would let her know that the band wanted to meet her backstage after the show and that she could bring a friend. We'd give our guests a tour backstage, offer them food, and then hang out and talk. I was never brave enough to do that, *and* I was always in a relationship, but the other guys did, and we met some pretty awesome people on the road. What made our lives different from the lives of a lot of other rock stars was that whatever happened backstage was typically pretty tame. It was fun hanging out with girls, but it wasn't about hookups or partying.

To have some fun during performances, we'd try to mix things up. Sometimes we'd dress up wearing fake mustaches and hats and camp out in the audience to see how long it would take for someone to recognize us. In Mexico that backfired, and the crowd got pretty rough with Logan. They really went nuts, and he thought they were going to tear his face off. When he finally made it backstage—in clothing that had been ripped by wild fans—he was legit terrified. So that was the end of that particular game.

Being onstage was a blast, singing, dancing, and doing stunts on a trampoline. Everything was timed down to the second: the costume changes, the lift that thrust all four of us onstage, and even the trampoline jumps. Even our wardrobe changes were epic. Each of us had a "changer," a girl from the crew who'd help us with wardrobe changes we had to pull off in forty-five seconds. We got it down to a science because we had to.

Though some of the outfits appeared to have buttons, there were no buttons or zippers, just Velcro. No matter what style of shoe we'd be wearing, they'd have a secret zipper up the side so that the whole shoe opened up for us to step out of it quickly. Our in-ear microphones were connected to small silicone packs sewed into our pants. So as we'd come offstage, someone would be grabbing those packs to transfer into our next costume. Hopping into that next pair of pants, we'd be back onstage in less than a minute. When my foot slipped while I was doing a backflip on one of the small trampolines, one of the springs cut my leg, but I kept singing as I felt warm blood oozing through my white pants.

And the show went on until the next wardrobe change—and then we kept going.

Once we had the show committed to memory, we really started having fun. We had a lot more freedom to joke around or mess up without worrying about getting every word right. Part of the choreography involved switching places on stage. So we'd rip the dirtiest farts so that the next guy had to slide into that wall of terrible. Then after the show we'd brag about our offerings and dish about who had it worst.

We'd gotten big in the United States, but what we experienced when we traveled to Central and South America was unreal. When tickets went on sale, venues with thirty thousand and even seventy-five thousand seats sold out.

When we'd move through these countries, we'd each be assigned a personal security guard from the United States and one local bodyguard who would be with us at all times when we were in public. The guards would wait outside our hotel rooms to shuttle us between venues.

When we arrived in Mexico and were waiting to pass through immigration lines, we were caught up in the same crush of travelers as every other passenger. But before long, people started looking at us and recognizing us. I glanced up at a second-story walkway to see the people waiting for arrivals begin to point and wave at us. The officials inspecting our passports started taking pictures with us. As our security crew tried to hustle us to get our baggage and exit the airport, mobs of fans followed us. Airport workers abandoned their jobs selling candy and newspapers to join the chaos. It was madness! At baggage claim girls hopped on the spinning carousel to try to get closer to us. Our handlers started grabbing our luggage and building a wall of bags around us. After strategizing, they found a way to open a side exit and helped us press through the crowds to exit the airport, leaving our bags behind. It was surreal.

Toward the end of the four-season show, the hours started to feel pretty brutal. Friday night we'd race to Chicago, do a show, and fly back Sunday to be ready to film Monday morning. The next Friday we'd start the whole cycle again, in Boston or Atlanta or Phoenix. It was a rough schedule.

On the red-eye flight one of us might ask, "Hey, guys, when's the next day off?"

And someone else would joke, "Dayuff? What's that? What's a Dayuff?"

We cracked us up.

After a few seasons our producer sat us down and asked, "What do you guys want to get out of this season?" He was giving us the opportunity to have some say in lives that were feeling more and more like they were being prescribed for us by others. The other three guys decided that they wanted to go to Coachella, so they asked to not work on Friday, and also to get Monday off. And it was done. Me? I thought they shot too low, so I asked to direct an episode of the show. And it was done! It was the one called "Big Time Tour Bus." And that opportunity qualified me for membership in the Directors Guild of America, a membership I continue to hold.

To the outside observer, I had it all. I was starring in a popular television show. I had adoring fans. I had money. I had cars. I was still dating a great girl. But I'd soon discover that I was missing what mattered most.

CHAPTER 2

INTRODUCING
CARMEN CORTEZ

LEX

During the earliest years of my life, I lived on a horse ranch in Ocala, Florida. When I was as young as three, my parents would put me on a four-wheeler, lock it into second gear, and let me use the throttle and brake to drive solo around the farm. Stall by stall, I'd scoop grain out of a bag anchored behind me and feed the horses. One of my earliest memories is flying through the barn on that four-wheeler!

On the farm I got to spend most of my time exploring outdoors, playing with critters, seeing horses being born, making mud pies, going fishing—there was always an adventure. Those few short years we spent there shaped the way I live my life today. My mom was just twenty years old when she had me, and she continued to travel the globe as a supermodel with a budding career. My mom was always adamant about keeping her kids close. So while it was unusual, she would bring us to every shoot, something I have always admired about her.

When I was four, my mom brought me with her on a trip to Los Angeles where she was doing a modeling shoot. My godmother,

Amy, who was also visiting LA with her nineteen-year-old daughter Cassidy, another model/actress, was watching me. While my mom was on the shoot, Amy took me to visit Hollywood. On our little adventure I saw the guy who was taking tourists' money for helping them press their hands into a square of wet cement to take home as a souvenir. The keepsakes were replicas of the brass stars embedded across fifteen blocks of sidewalk on Hollywood Boulevard honoring the entertainment industry's biggest stars. Though I didn't yet understand the significance of those sidewalk squares, I did want to put my hand in some squishy cement, and Amy let me do it. That night I proudly presented the cement square to my mom. In my earliest years she was very physically affectionate and incredibly encouraging. She always made us feel so special, and she acted impressed by my offering.

Amy's daughter had agents in Hollywood and took us with her when she went to meet with them. During that brief visit a representative from the agency—*that did not represent children*—told Amy and my mom that they wanted to represent me. I had always loved people's reactions when I would entertain them, so I imagine they must've seen some spark in me.

These amazing agents, Ro Diamond and Suzy Schwartz, immediately pitched me to a casting director for the family-friendly show *Evening Shade*, which starred Burt Reynolds as a retired professional football player who had moved back to his hometown of the same name. They basically pressured her, "We think it's time for the baby on your show to grow up," convincing her to consider a child for the role the following season. When the new season started, it would be as if a few years had passed and the baby had become a four-year-old.

With my mom's permission, I ended up having two auditions that week. Because the scene that Mom and Amy had helped me learn lines for depended on my having a doll and we didn't have one on hand, I made one out of tissue, roped together with elastic hair bands, for the scene.

Though I had no idea who this guy named Burt Reynolds was, in my second audition I ran lines with him. Following the audition Burt stooped down, looked into my eyes, and said, "Alexa, I really want you to be on my show."

I saw Amy's face light up at his words, but I wasn't yet on board.

I told him coolly, "I'll have to think about it."

He looked baffled by my response but then started laughing pretty hard and answered, "I *told you* I want you to be on the show."

"I told you, Burt," I retorted, "I just have to think about it."

His wide-eyed look told me he wasn't used to people speaking to him like that.

When my mom brought me to her modeling shoots, I was intrigued by the world of entertainment and was always ready to perform. So she was delighted for me and knew I'd end up in acting.

As you might guess, this fast-track path isn't the way things typically happen in this industry. Especially to be a regular on a television series. More often, actors audition countless times before various people, then there are callbacks, then there's a read with the director, then a studio test, then a network test. Landing a role on a TV series should have been a much more elaborate process, so I was fortunate for the unlikely opportunity I was offered.

But my opportunity meant changes for my family.

When I was offered the role on *Evening Shade*, we were living in Florida, and my mom wasn't willing to split up the family. Just as she'd always taken my younger sister Krizia and me on modeling shoots with her, now our family would relocate to Los Angeles for me to pursue acting. But prior to relocating, my family moved to Puerto Rico for six months to sell off the horses from our ranch. When we finally arrived in LA, we stayed at the infamous Oakwood Apartments—sandwiched between Boyz II Men and Christina Milian!

My first day on set was like entering a whole new reality. On the set of a sitcom, everything is in a little box, which is the room in which filming is happening in front of four cameras. Think of it like a play: the actors in sitcoms perform facing toward the cameras so viewers don't see that flying overhead are floating microphones. To my four-year-old gaze, they looked like *puppets*. I was so intrigued by them that the directors had to instruct me not to look up. So the first lesson I ever learned on set was that I couldn't look at floating puppets.

While the set seemed so foreign on that first day, the homey living room and kitchen would quickly become the place where I felt most comfortable. It's where my people were: family, cast, and crew. It's where I did the majority of my schoolwork. Sometimes it would be on the set of a studio in Los Angeles, and other times it would be on location. Being on set quickly became home for me.

When the show concluded I got to attend my first Hollywood party. The Sportsmen's Lodge in the Valley was decorated to the hilt for the glamorous evening. What most captured my imagination were miniature confetti stars sprinkled all over the tables.

As I reached out to touch the glimmering gold and silver stars, I was certain that *real stars* had fallen out of the night sky and landed on the table where I was seated. And, savvy girl that I was, I filled an entire plastic cup with them and kept them in my closet for . . . longer than I care to admit. (Let's keep that our secret, okay?)

After two seasons on the show, I said goodbye to my on-screen family. Then a year later, when I was seven with *two* younger sisters, my parents divorced. That thing for which I always yearned, that feeling of home, was broken—though I'd continue to find home on various sets. I also longed for relationships with peers. Not long after the divorce, my sisters and I moved with my mom to Canyon Country, California, where I met my *one* friend, Sabrina, who lived two houses down from me. Sabrina and I made make-believe adventures in the backyard. We collected and traded an impressive array of glossy, glittery stickers. And, as savvy entrepreneurs, we gathered pine cones and rocks from the neighborhood and sold them door to door. (Those stickers weren't going to pay for themselves.) And although we only lived in that neighborhood for a few years, Sabrina became a lifelong friend.

My favorite project I ever worked on was a movie I made when I was eleven called *Run the Wild Fields*. It was filmed about an hour outside of Toronto, where the landscape reminded me of the sweet time when our family lived on the ranch in Florida. My mom and both my sisters, Krizia and Makenzie, were with me during shooting. And when I'd finish for the day, I loved spending time with them. That shoot will always stand out to me as one of the happiest memories I have with my family.

My eleventh year was also when we began to lose touch with

my dad, whose story could be made into a blockbuster movie. A Colombian American, he worked undercover for the US Drug Enforcement Administration (DEA), busting drug traffickers— and that's all I am allowed to say on that. As jarring as many find this revelation today, as a girl I was completely clueless. I hadn't known what my dad's job was. I didn't know he was putting people in jail. Sheltered from it all, I was just a kid enjoying life.

I'm not completely clear on how the drug-bust business works, but years later something went awry and my dad went to prison for over a year. By the time I was twelve, my mom had grown more concerned about the risk my dad's work posed to her girls and had started to cut him out of our lives.

My mom didn't play when it came to her babies. She would do whatever it took to protect us, even if it was from our dad. She was pretty strict and held the reins tight. She always said that if you give kids a boundary, they will push it and step beyond it, so she made sure her boundaries were close and tight! I learned quickly that her no meant no. "No, you're not allowed to act this way." If I got sassy during an acting gig, she had no problem pulling me off the job. She'd seen the train-wreck stories of other child actors, and she'd decided that her child was going to be respectful and a good kid or I wouldn't remain part of the industry. While some kids my age would have loved to be cut loose from *their* jobs—babysitting or mowing lawns—to me, being pulled off a job felt like my *home* had been ripped away from me. So the looming threat kept me in line. My sisters and I had strict rules, but we were good kids. And considering the business we were growing up in, my mom managed to keep our lives pretty normal.

She was also thoughtful about the roles I took. When I was offered a role that would have me practicing magic as a witch, we passed on it. My mom's heart, and the intention I also shared, was to honor God. During my childhood she'd taken me to church every week, at Shepherd of the Hills in Northridge, California, and I wanted my own faith to be as important to me as hers was to her.

I was shocked when my mom let me go to a three-day weekend church camp when I was nine, because she'd always kept me so close. Because I was hungry for the friendships typical kids enjoy, it was an epic weekend for me. And since the movies I'd done to that point hadn't yet made me recognizable, I spent three days as a totally normal kid. And I thought normal was awesome. While I now suspect that neither Mom nor I had yet fully met the God who knew us and loved us, I do think that God honored us because we purposed to honor Him.

A few years after my parents divorced, when I was ten, my mom started dating Eric, whom I've always considered to be my stepdad. He isn't *legally* my stepdad, since he and my mom never married. I believe the difficulties in her first marriage caused her to be cautious of marrying again. But Eric is the man I remember raising me, along with my mom. He did the grocery shopping, the cooking, and the dishes and fixed anything that needed to be fixed around our home. He was the father figure who was there for me during my childhood. Imagine being a guy who was willing to take on a woman with three kids! At the time I didn't realize how big that was, but it makes me appreciate him so much more now. He was so good to all of us.

At the same time, I was crushed when my mom became pregnant with Eric's child. Because she'd always instilled in me that God wanted us to save ourselves for our husbands, I was hurt and disappointed to find out that she was pregnant. Concerned that they'd slept together outside of marriage, and naively convinced it had been just one time, I got tangled up in a huge fight with her. My heart filled with confusion, I remember sobbing on the bathroom floor, unable to look at her.

"How could you do that?!" I begged. "You'll probably slip up and do it again!"

And while I think I'd handle it differently today, and certainly did handle it differently when welcoming my two half brothers by Eric into our family, I'd come by my resistance up to that point honestly, as it had been my *mom* who'd instilled those values in me. It was confusing to me, and I didn't understand. She'd told me one thing but lived another. The ease of the relationship my mom and I had enjoyed when I was younger, like so many mothers and daughters, morphed into a trickier one during my adolescence.

After *Run the Wild Fields*, I auditioned for a movie called *Spy Kids*, along with every other kid in Hollywood. In my mind it was just another audition for another movie. No big deal. When I walked into the audition, as an eleven-year-old, I noticed that the director had a super cool vibe. He was wearing a headband and playing a guitar.

I called him out: "You seem like a kid. You don't seem like an old dude."

Thankfully, he laughed.

My audition went great, but the producers thought I was too old for the part. Thinking forward, they wanted to find an actress who could age with the movie if there was a sequel. So I had to audition for *Spy Kids* six times, again and again, the same scenes over and over again. Finally, it was the big test day when you know you're in the finals and they do a camera test.

In one of the few times our family split up, my mom had accompanied my little sister Makenzie to film *The Family Man* with Nicolas Cage in New York. So my stepdad Eric brought me to the *Spy Kids* test. What stands out about that day is that it was the first time my hair had ever been straightened on set. I know you'd think my lasting memory would be something more significant, like the meaning of that day or the pressure I might have felt. Nope. I was a kid who was excited someone straightened my hair! The job had come down to three finalists, and we were all rooting for one another. I've never had much of a competitive streak. At the end of the day I felt good about my performance, but I also knew they were still hesitant about my "old" age.

That Christmas we visited all three sets of grandparents in Florida. I didn't yet know if I'd gotten the role, but I was too busy creating some of my warmest childhood memories at my grandparents' houses, my Nana and her husband, DC; my Papa and his wife, Jill; and my dad's mother, Yeya, who'd lost her husband when I was three. We saw them for holidays and other family gatherings, and because they all got along so well and lived near one another, I was usually around all of them at the same time.

Nana had a house on the St. John's River with a dock, so we spent hours out there fishing and playing. On the Colombian side of my family, my dad was one of twelve kids and lived like they were still in Colombia, my abuelita Yeya not even bothering to learn English. When she passed, she had ninety-six grandkids and great grandkids. (Yup, I've got ninety-five Colombian cousins.) I still remember playing with an endless stream of cousins as the smells of *sancocho* and *arroz con pollo* wafted through their home.

But we were at my Nana's house for Christmas when I got the call that I'd been chosen to be Carmen Cortez in *Spy Kids*. I learned that the director, Robert Rodriguez, the guy who didn't act like an old person, had really gone to bat for me to get the role. (I made sure to thank him when we started shooting two months later!) Interestingly, the producers wanted me to look more traditionally Latina for the role of Carmen. Colombians come in all different colors: pale-skinned and dark-skinned, light hair and dark hair, but because Daryl Sabara, my on-screen brother Juni, was a redhead and of Polish and Russian descent, they wanted me to have dark hair. I was fine with that change; I thought it was cool. My mom had always let Krizia put blue and red streaks in her dark hair, but I was never allowed to experiment because I was working.

When I was filming *Spy Kids*, I didn't yet have a real-life brother, so Daryl, who was eight, became my surrogate younger brother. We'd be goofing around, playing with the cool gadgets, and he would purposely try to annoy me, which he doesn't deny. I was constantly mad at him the way an older sister naturally would be. (Mind you, I wouldn't let anyone else pick on him, but I could.) We'd fight with each other while hanging out on set, but we loved each other *so much*. We still do today.

Before the film was released, I was sent to do mall signings across the United States in conjunction with an Isuzu campaign, since Isuzus were the vehicles used in the movie. Though the movie posters had been released, nobody had a clue who I was. Maybe two people at some random mall who felt bad seeing me sitting there alone would stop by to ask me to sign pity autographs.

Once the film was released, however, everything changed. During a press junket, Daryl and I might sit in a room for eight hours and have a hundred different interviewers pummeling us with questions. Some were given three minutes, some were given ten, every one of them asking the same questions. By the time we showed up at the Mall of America to sign autographs, fifteen thousand people had shown up! And only three thousand of them got autographs.

The excitement of filming the movie, though, made up for having to do press. I'd always loved being on *any* set, but the sets for *Spy Kids* truly were as fantastic as they seem on screen. Talented designers had crafted our safehouse, and Floop's crazy castle, and these huge cave tunnels. It was so fun to inhabit those scenes, play with props, and basically play the ultimate dress-up game every day.

After *Spy Kids* was released, we quickly realized that it wasn't just another movie. It was special. Robert, the director, describes it as Willy-Wonka-meets-James-Bond. It was a surprise hit, grossing over $147 million. With its success we were soon back in the studio filming *Spy Kids 2: Island of Lost Dreams* (I tried to figure out how to not visibly age during those months).

While the cast on *Spy Kids* was just adults with the only kids being Daryl, me, and our stunt doubles, more kids joined us when we filmed the sequel. Matthew O'Leary and Emily Osment joined the cast, bringing with them more stunt doubles and new stand-ins, who helped block out scenes before we shot each one. It was a lot of kids, and I absolutely *loved* it. The nature of my childhood, moving from show to show and set to set, had made it hard to develop consistent friendships, and suddenly I was surrounded by more kids than I could count.

One day we found a room that wasn't being used, busted open the lock, and made it into a break-dance room. Some of my friends at school were into hip-hop, and the next natural expression for our youthful exuberance was break-dancing. We put cardboard down, turned up the Rio Diamond, an early MP3 player, and showed off our break-dancing and hip-hop moves to Gigi D'Agostino's "Fly With Me" and a lot of Linkin Park. I think we were fortunate to not have had the distraction of social media back then, because it allowed us to be present in the moment. And we had some really good moments. We didn't spend a lot of time dwelling on the success of the film; we were just having a blast being together. I couldn't have asked for more in that season of my life.

Those kids were like my brothers and sisters. And in so many ways, the *Spy Kids* cast and crew became like family to me. The crew weren't just nameless people doing hair and makeup or working cameras. They were the people I spent every day with, who knew me and cared about me. From the prop team to the stunt team, everyone felt like family. Danny Trejo, who played Carmen and Juni's on-screen uncle, became *my* uncle. Although he was that rough and tough character, Danny is truly the sweetest guy. To this day he'll leave me voice messages singing "My Sweet Angel" or insisting that if I don't call him back immediately, he will stab himself in the eye with a sharp object. (Funny, right?)

When asked, I pretty much always rave about how dreamy the experience was. But recently someone asked me what the *hardest* part was about *Spy Kids*. Honestly? The *parents*. The parents of the child actors always seemed to have issues with each other that kept us from being able to hang out as much as we'd have liked. We wanted to spend time together after hours, but because a lot of these parents had beefs with each other off set, we had our playtime between filming scenes. (And sneaking off to the break-dance room when we broke for meals!) And this was why a lot of us hated the weekends. We wanted to be hanging out with other kids, and we didn't get those opportunities.

Another reason weekends stunk is because we'd often have to catch up on our schoolwork. Industry rules dictated that we needed to accomplish three hours of schoolwork every day on set, and if we didn't reach that, we'd have to make it up at some point. If we logged five hours on Monday, we'd only need to do one the next day. And if we could "bank" hours, getting ahead, the producers had more flexibility with what and when we could shoot. So we'd power through our friendless homework weekends and look forward to getting back to the set on Monday. Luckily I had the coolest on-set teacher, Pat Jackson, who traveled with me for years. Mr. Pat helped instill in me a love for math and a good balance of work and play!

Unlike some of the other kids on set, I did have my sisters with me, Krizia and Makenzie (and my younger sister Greylin, during the second *Spy Kids*). Steve and Kaylah, the movie's prop team, *adored* my little sisters. They'd invite them into the prop shop to teach them how to make their own outdoor ovens to bake clay pots! Krizia and Makenzie had a ball. When we filmed some of the scenes in an abandoned airport hangar, the producers hired a Fun Coordinator to keep the crew of kids on set entertained, so my sisters got to join in Silly String wars, water-balloon fights, cake-throwing fights, and more. (Best job ever, right?) Feel free to imagine fifteen kids covered in chocolate cake. It was absolutely as delicious as it sounds.

For *Island of Lost Dreams* we got to shoot in beautiful Costa Rica. We filmed under waterfalls and even at the base of an active volcano that rumbled like an earthquake one day. We wondered if the volcano was going to explode, and I remember seeing Kaylah running for her life, thinking it was the end! Critics can say what they will about the plight of poor, overworked child actors, but for me it was an amazing experience for which I'm so grateful. I would have filmed *ten* of these movies if they let me!

For the first *Spy Kids*, Daryl and I went through stunt boot camp. We learned gymnastics stunts, fighting skills, and more. Though professional stunt kids would test out some of the stunts ahead of filming, Daryl and I did most of our own stunts on that set.

The stunt kids did more of the stunts on the second film, but I did get to do a pretty amazing scene in Lajitas, Texas, where we were filming right off the Rio Grande on a rock formation that jutted out to a point over a drop of about eight hundred feet. In that scene I am fighting these evil skeletons, and a flying creature picks me up and takes me away. The crew was going to use a crane to lift me off the rock and fly me off this scary cliff, but our amazing stunt team designed this original setup with picks in the rock that I could be safely harnessed to while I was also securely attached to a crane from the top. Super safe, right? But for the shot, they'd unharness me from the rock.

On that day, when we were between setups, we heard a loud creaking. The crane, which wasn't well-balanced, began to tip over. What was most wild is that it was suddenly silent except for the sound of the crane. With over a hundred crew members working under it, there should have been screaming. But there was just eerie creaking and then a giant crash as the crane fell on its side. I'm so grateful I wasn't hooked to it at that moment.

It was a miracle that no one died. We finished the scene on a green-screen set in Austin.

I was a youthful thirteen when we were filming *Spy Kids 2*, and I started "dating" my first boyfriend, Nick, one of the stunt kids. I say "dating" because I wasn't allowed to have a boyfriend and this was the first slightly sneaky thing I ever did. I still vividly remember how my heart fluttered when I saw him, those feelings of first love. Nick was the first boy to kiss me, and we'd date on and off—in secret!—for the next six years. (And Makenzie even dated his brother Jake after Nick and I broke up.)

Nick and I were still secret-dating during *Spy Kids 3D: Game Over*. That movie used cool 3D effects, and movie theater audiences were given red-and-blue 3D glasses when they purchased their tickets. Even the DVD release included four sets of glasses.

I suppose anyone from the outside would look at my career and assume I was financially successful. But honestly, I didn't deal with it, I didn't think about it, and I didn't care a lot about it. I wasn't obsessed with money because I saw what it did to people. I trusted God, and I knew that God had taken care of my family and taken care of me.

In 2006, when I turned eighteen and was old enough to move out, I wasn't given any money to do so. My mom reasoned that because it seemed like I'd really never considered the acting I'd done to be work, then I probably wasn't expecting the financial benefits that had accompanied it. This actually didn't bother me much because I knew that everyone in my family had sacrificed for me to do what I loved. My mom forfeited opportunities. She negotiated deals on my behalf. My siblings didn't attend normal schools, so they missed the friendships, birthday parties, and dances that would have accompanied normal schooling. A large part of me felt like I owed all of them. And while others were offended by what they believed to be a slight to me, I honestly didn't care about the money. My family had made my career possible, and for that I was grateful.

So at eighteen, when I moved out of my mom's home, I left with nothing. Thankfully my friend Kaley Cuoco, from *The Big Bang Theory*, let me live on her couch. When I booked my first job as an eighteen-year-old, a movie called *Broken Hill* that was being filmed in Australia, I was "working" for the first time.

It was a lonelier season for me. But ever since I was a kid, I'd had a strong sense that God was with me, and I'd been seeking a relationship with Him. I journaled my thoughts and prayers like I was having a real conversation with God. Many times I really had to lean on that relationship. Throughout our early years, my mom would tell my sisters and me that we were bad kids, and at some level we believed it. We knew we weren't *terrible*, but we figured we must have been some kind of bad.

Though we've not revisited this, I suspect she said things she regrets today. So I'd beg God to help me be a better kid because I didn't want to keep messing up and making my mom mad at me. Some days it felt like I couldn't say or do anything right. Looking back, I think I was so worried there was going to be an issue that my tiptoeing around my mom ended up *causing* an issue.

I'm convinced that we come into this world with a desire for God. We're *born* to want Him. We're tempted to quench it, and so we feed that hunger with many other things, but that longing was always with me. Although my mom stopped taking us to church when I was about twelve, I continued to go when I could as a teen, and when I turned sixteen, I was able to drive myself. Though I'd eventually discover that God had much more in store for me than I could yet imagine, all along I knew that He was holding me in His care. Although I couldn't entirely understand it, I could feel His presence with me.

CHAPTER 3

"WHY ARE YOU SO HAPPY?"

LOS

Don't be stupid."

During the third season of *Big Time Rush*, when the boys were buying cool sports cars, I decided I wanted to buy something fancy.

When I announced my intentions to buy a sweet ride to my dad on the phone one evening, he said without hesitation, "Don't be stupid. Real estate makes more sense. Increases in value. Let's buy something together."

And while that sounded super boring to me, and not nearly as fun as a Beemer, the seed had been planted. A few weeks later I was hanging out with my friend Francia Raisa at her place, and she was talking about changes she wanted to make to her home.

"Are you renting?" I asked, curious.

"No," she explained patiently. "I own it."

As a twenty-year-old, the concept boggled my mind. "Wait, you can *own* it?!" I asked, incredulous.

Francia laughed.

"How do you *own* this?!" I begged to know.

Not wanting to take the time to download all of *Real Estate for Dummies*, she answered, "Here, just call my friend. I'm sending you his contact info. Call Andrew Mortaza."

Three days later Andrew and I were sharing a pitcher of margaritas on the patio of Mexicali, a restaurant on Ventura Boulevard. I told him what I was looking for and the budget on which my dad and I had agreed.

"Cool," Andrew agreed. "I'll get on it."

The next day Andrew sent me a number of listings featuring the cool kind of bachelor pad I'd described to him. In the meantime, however, my dad had found a three-story, seven-thousand-square-foot mansion in the flats of Encino that looked like it had belonged to some shady drug lord. And it was pink. No joke. *Pink!* Nothing about it screamed cool bachelor pad.

When I sent Andrew the listing, he was baffled.

"You *want* this?" he asked.

I understood why he was confused. "I don't," I explained, "but my dad says this is the one."

My dad's dream was to be able to give each of his four sons a house. And I was suddenly at the top of the list. He made an offer and, because he'd recently done well in the stock market, was able to put down a lot of cash. We closed thirty days later. The deal we made was that he'd buy it, and I'd put the energy, hours, and dollars into fixing it up. It needed a *lot* of work. Complete makeover.

So Andrew walked us through the purchase process, and I spent the next two years on the reno project. During that season I was in two relationships. And although I'm not particularly proud of it, I really did move from one relationship to the next.

It wasn't that I had a *lot* of girlfriends. I didn't. But because I'd move from one to the next, I was never single.

When I first got to Los Angeles, I'd continued dating Cassie, whom I'd met in college. She loved Jesus and had even taken me to her family's Baptist church in Mississippi. She had me singing worship songs before I knew what a worship song even was! At that time I didn't even understand who Jesus was because I hadn't encountered Him yet for myself. Through FaceTime calls and weekend visits, Cassie and I continued a cross-country relationship.

While Cassie and I were together, like the dumb twenty-year-old guy I was, I started talking to Sam—a girl I'd met when she came to see Big Time Rush in Las Vegas. She'd actually come to see her good friend Kendall perform, but she and I clicked. Sam and I started hanging out back in LA, and when things started getting serious, I didn't tell Cassie. When Cassie tried to call me one day and I wasn't picking up, she called me even more. She then called James and Logan and Kendall to find out where I was. When Sam asked who was calling me so much, I lied to her and said it was a spam caller. Then, because I turned off my phone and kept it off until noon the next day, I lied again to Cassie!

"You're not going to believe this, Cass," I bluffed, when I called her the day after Sam and I went out. "I had my phone last night, and then it was gone! I spent all night looking for it. So this morning I had to buy a new phone and a new case!"

When I texted her a picture of my "new phone," she recognized the same case I'd always used. Gaslighting her, I insisted, "You know I love that case! I was lucky to find the *same one*."

Things with Cassie had been strained, and I knew the relationship wasn't going to last. I didn't like being alone, though, so I wanted to have someone else lined up before Cassie and I were over. I never *cheated*, but I was already opening the Sam door as I was closing the Cassie door. After I broke up with Cassie, having made her think it was her idea, I started dating Sam.

I was a mess. I was. And looking back, I'm embarrassed at how I treated these sweet girls. But I would have done anything to avoid having to confront and deal with the truth.

The second year Sam and I dated, she started going to a Bible study. And, in some twist of fate, it met at Andrew's house—yes, my real estate agent. (Weird, right?) Sam was growing in her faith, and she kept inviting me to this Bible study. I said no every time. I'd been raised going to the Catholic church with my mom, and even had my first Communion, but I did not identify as a particularly religious or spiritual person. Later, when my mom and dad were really struggling in their marriage, we started going to a Baptist church that was supposed to help them. When it didn't, the experience left a sour taste in my mouth for religion. It was fine for other people—like Cassie, for whom I had mad respect—but it wasn't for me. Going to something like Bible study was definitely for religious nuts.

Sam and I were together for two years, and she even moved into the beautifully renovated pink drug lord house with me. When our relationship became strained, however, we broke up. And when I say that we broke up, I mean that I was *done*, didn't have the courage to break up with her, and manipulated her into breaking up with me.

"You seem angry. If you're so mad at me," I pressed, "just be done with this. Let's just end this, because you're so mad."

Manipulative, right?

But, like my other relationships, I didn't force the end until I had someone else in my sights. (I know, I was terrible.) I was already kind of crushing on a girl who'd been in a Big Time Rush video that the band filmed in Hawaii. So in her I could see an open door, and after Sam and I broke up, I even started spending time with this girl. But during that summer, I realized that Sam was the girl for me. I broke up with the video girl and tried to get back with Sam, texting her all summer. But she wasn't having it. And when I didn't have a girlfriend at all, which hadn't happened since I started dating in high school, I began to unravel.

Feeling miserable, I started smoking weed. I even tried shrooms once. That summer we'd be in a different city every day. After our shows we'd sometimes get invited to hang out and party with people we knew or we'd met, but when I think of my rock-bottom moments, I see myself sitting on that tour bus, stoned, having eaten a tub of ice cream. If I wasn't out having fun, I'd just zone out and watch *Game of Thrones*.

At the end of the summer, after the tour was over, I'd lock myself in the home theater I'd built in my spacious home and smoke weed. I'd only leave the theater to grab food when DoorDash arrived with my pizza or Chinese food. I'd never been a big drinker, but that summer I drank a lot as well. I didn't reach out to family or friends for help. Instead I holed up at home and wallowed in my pain. Opening the door to my big empty home, I stepped inside and was alone again.

My breakup with Sam had triggered a larger crisis inside me, and I was asking big questions for which I had no answers:

- *What am I doing?*
- *What does it all even mean?*
- *What's the point?*

For three years I'd been on top of the world. I'd been happy with Cass and then Sam. I drove really cool cars. I had money to buy whatever I wanted. I had adoring fans. I literally lived in a freaking *mansion*. But I was empty, and I didn't know what it was that I was missing. I tried to fill that void with girlfriends, toys, houses, whatever was new on Amazon, and eventually weed. But when Sam and I broke up, and I spiraled downward, I had a reality check. None of those things had satisfied. None filled me in the way I thought they might.

While I was still wallowing in that pit of despair, I happened to think about the real estate agent who'd helped my dad and me buy the house—Andrew, who'd been hosting the Bible study Sam had attended. Though we weren't close, Andrew and I had stayed in touch after buying the house, speaking every few months. There was something different about him that I couldn't quite put my finger on. For starters, he was always happy. And while I know that others would likely have guessed the same about me, I could see that Andrew's peace and contentment ran deep. He was generous. He was honest. He was kind. He was consistent.

During one of my evening binges, I dialed Andrew.

"Hey man," he greeted me when he picked up.

I cut to the chase. "Why are you so happy?" I queried.

"What?" he asked, having no idea what I was talking about.

"What is it?" I prodded. "Why are you so happy?"

His answer was one I was unprepared to receive. "Jesus," he answered simply.

Had we been in the same room, he would have seen my eyes roll dramatically to the back of my head.

As Andrew continued to share why Jesus made a difference in his life, I listened politely but wasn't really paying attention. Before we ended our conversation that evening, we agreed to get together face-to-face soon. But at two in the morning, after hauling myself to my bedroom and collapsing into bed, I continued to think about what Andrew had shared. The next day after work, I called him again.

When Andrew answered, I blurted, "Okay, talk to me about it."

After sharing for a little bit, Andrew invited me to join him at church on Sunday. I can only assume that, sensing both my despair and my resistance, he realized he needed reinforcements. So with more curiosity than I'd had before, I reluctantly agreed to meet him at his church Sunday morning.

Andrew's family had fled from Afghanistan when he was three and made a new life in the United States as refugees. His parents and all his siblings were Muslim, but Andrew met Christ at the age of twenty-eight and has been on fire every day since then. He's this Middle Eastern guy who's about ten years older than I am. Always smiling. So whatever church you're imagining we attended, it's probably not Andrew's church.

The address Andrew gave me for Harvest Christian Center was in the South Bay region of LA county, not too far from the airport. The nine-square-mile neighborhood, Inglewood, was historically white in the 1950s and '60s but at the time was about 80 percent Black and Latino. Finding a parking spot on the street, I spotted Andrew waiting in front of the church for me.

As we passed through the front doors that had been flung open to welcome all, a Black woman about my mom's age welcomed me with a huge smile and a hug. An usher inside greeted us warmly and walked us to a pew in the middle of the room. Throughout the small church I saw women wearing large, colorful hats, and little girls and boys in their best Sunday outfits. In my jeans and hoodie, I was definitely underdressed. Parents held babies, siblings snuggled together, and a few men in suits, holding leather Bibles and sitting in red velvet chairs, flanked the preacher who sat enthroned behind the raised pulpit. Light glowed through the colorful stained glass windows on both sides of the sanctuary.

After some hand-clapping and foot-stomping songs that I couldn't *not* enjoy, the choir sang "Break Every Chain." As the organ music wound down, an elder made a few announcements and prayed before inviting the pastor, introduced as "Bishop," to share the morning message.

When Bishop Ganther stepped to the pulpit, I braced myself. Yeah, the worship time had been awesome, but I wasn't sure I was ready for some preacher to get preachy on me. So I kind of erected a personal invisible force field to shield me from whatever religious talk was about to make me feel even worse than I already did for the lifestyle I'd been living. I checked out mentally when he began by reading from the Bible. I can't even tell you what text he preached from. So imagine my surprise when, halfway through his message, Bishop announced, "I was twenty-three once."

Wait, what? Is he talking to me? Because I'm twenty-three!

"And when I was twenty-three, I was smoking the doobies . . ."

Warmth flushed across my face, and I was sure that everyone in the congregation knew he was talking to me.

"I'd come to church with a bottle of Jack in the back of the car," he confessed.

I didn't have a bottle of Jack, but the point still hit home. *Yeah, I'm still listening . . .*

"I was sleeping around . . ."

Me too.

And then Bishop proceeded to share how he'd met Jesus, been forgiven of his sins, and given his life to serve the Lord. With every word I felt the heavy burden of depression and despair and confusion lifting off my shoulders. If Jesus could redeem Bishop, then Jesus could redeem me.

After the service I had the opportunity to shake Bishop's hand at the door and tell him how much his message had meant to me. I know I was beaming like one of these goofy religious people, and I felt like a completely different person. I joined Andrew and we drove to meet up with his family for lunch at Santa Monica pier. And I was on a Jesus high!

"Andrew," I told him in the car, "this is what I want to do. This is what I want to be about. I want to live like that guy. And like you. I want to start fresh!"

Andrew, smiling, confirmed that I was making the decision of my life, and he invited me to Bible study at his house on Thursday night. Yeah, the one Sam went to. And with the new hope that had been born in my heart, I began to dream about the possibility of meeting up with her and getting back together.

As we drove, I kept thinking about Bishop's message and the ways he shared that he'd hurt others when he was living his life before he met Jesus. And I suddenly felt convicted to apologize to every person I'd ever wronged in my lifetime.

The list wasn't short.

At the restaurant I said a quick hello to Andrew's family and then stepped outside to start calling random people from my contacts. Guys and girls I hadn't spoken to in years were all on my list. I never even ordered or ate a meal. I was just outside for two hours calling people who were shocked to hear from me.

"Hey," I'd begin. "This is Carlos Pena. Not sure if you remember me, but I know I lied to you about a few things, and I just want you to know I'm really sorry."

I called Cassie to apologize for how I treated her at the end of our relationship.

I called all my siblings.

I called people from high school (some of them did not even remember me).

If I'd teased someone, or if we'd been in a fight, or if I'd bailed on them somehow, they got a call. I felt a deep pull inside to right every wrong I'd committed in my twenty-three years. Friends and family members who picked up their phones that afternoon were usually a little surprised, but most accepted my apology. They may have thought I was crazy when they hung up, but all of them were pretty cool to me on the phone.

When I finally rolled into the garage of my house that night, I felt like a different person. My first stop was my bedroom, where I kept my stash of weed. I'd seen what integrity looked like as I'd watched Andrew's life, and I sensed that same commitment in the people I'd met at Harvest Christian Center. So I flushed all my weed down the toilet. I was ready to start living a life that honored Jesus.

When I showed up at Andrew's house four days later, I was all in. I wanted to grow in my faith, and I knew that Andrew could help me do that.

And if I'm honest, part of me was really psyched to see Sam again.

During Bible study I had the opportunity to share my testimony, and afterward I connected with Sam and sat beside her, sort of cuddly, on Andrew's kitchen counter. It was her birthday, and the following day she was going to Vegas for a girls' weekend. The vibe felt good, and I was hopeful that we were getting back together.

During the social hangout time after Bible study, Andrew had to dip out to pick up some girl who was supposed to have come to Bible study but had gotten a flat tire on the way. And while I was talking to Sam in the kitchen, I saw him walk in with this beautiful girl, about five feet tall. Without even thinking, I jumped off the counter and walked up to the two of them.

Extending my hand, I said, "Hey, how are you? My name's Carlos."

The curly-haired beauty replied, "I'm Alexa, nice to meet you."

Turning to Alexa, Andrew interjected, "He's the one I was telling you about."

They'd been talking about me? I didn't hate that. Andrew had known Alexa since she was fifteen and had recently mentioned to her that she and I would probably hit it off.

Then I got real chatty, told her how I was on *Big Time Rush*, learned that she'd been in *Spy Kids*, and talked about like one hundred other things as well. When she got a call that the tow truck driver had arrived a few blocks away, she and Andrew returned to his car for him to drive her back.

I said goodbye as they dipped, but a few moments after they left, I knew there was one more thing to say. Dashing out to Andrew's car, I knocked on his window for him to roll it down.

As the window dropped, I hollered, "Oh, *shiitake mushrooms*!"

It was a line from *Spy Kids*. When I'd watched it, I had been unimpressed. But somehow, in that moment, it felt like the right thing to shout in her face.

Alexa's wide-eyed expression said what her mouth did not: "This guy is such a weirdo." She wasn't wrong.

She seemed like a cool girl, and I was glad I'd met her. At the end of the evening, though, I was still feeling good about reconnecting with Sam.

When I gave Sam a ride home that night, sure that I was her dude again, I bid her goodbye, saying, "See you on Monday!" And because I remembered that she had been wanting a bike for a while, the day after Bible study I went to the bike store and bought her a purple beach cruiser. She loved it.

Because I felt like *all* the pieces had *magically* fallen into place for us to get back together, I was crushed when she didn't text or call me all weekend from Vegas. *What is happening? Am I misreading the obvious signals that she is into me?* Maybe I was.

In the next few weeks, my life started to look different to others. I started worshiping regularly at Andrew's church, which quickly became *my* church, and I even joined the choir. (Yes, you should absolutely imagine this Latino boy surrounded by a sea of well-dressed African Americans singing in a gospel choir.) Although I didn't plan to, after I encountered Jesus in Inglewood, I stopped cursing. Those ugly words just didn't feel right in my mouth anymore. Family and friends noticed too. I stopped drinking and smoking. And I had *loved* the feeling of getting high, chilling, and eating delicious food. I'd obviously known it wasn't the greatest choice, but that empty space inside me had craved it. But after meeting Christ, that craving was gone. I even had a respite from craving sex! For a while. I started tithing at church, giving 10 percent of my income to Harvest Christian Center, which I never would have even considered doing before.

The day I submitted my life to Jesus and decided to follow him, my life took a 180-degree turn. None of it was by my own strength; it really was God's power at work in my life in ways that I didn't completely understand.

Jesus had become the most important person in my life. But someone else was about to roar into my world as a close second.

CHAPTER 4

INSECURE

LEX

Being voted one of *Vanity Fair*'s hottest teen celebrities at age fourteen seems like it would have been the magic sauce to boost the confidence and self-image of any teenage girl, right?

One would think so. But on the day of the photo shoot, featuring a host of other teens, I was having all the regular self-conscious feels and noticings that any other teen would have.

I hadn't eaten and felt bloated.

I felt awkward around other teens I admired and was meeting for the first time.

My hair had been dyed dark for a movie, and I wished it was my natural, lighter color since I was being featured as "Alexa" and not my character "Carmen."

Like every other fourteen-year-old girl, I wanted to fit in.

For my freshman year of high school, after filming *Spy Kids 3*, I was normal. Ish. I had begged my mom to let me attend regular school, so I began attending a private Catholic school called Notre Dame High School in Sherman Oaks. Like any other kid starting high school, I was terrified to show up in my plaid uniform on the first day, knowing almost nobody. It is hard enough going to a new school as an incoming freshman with zero friends. Now add the fact that I was a "Spy Kid" starting high school. I was immediately the butt of all jokes.

I showed up at school that first week as myself—regular tomboy Alexa, without fancy hair or makeup. I quickly realized these LA girls were serious about grooming themselves to look like grown women. Before then I had no idea girls my age spent so much time doing their hair and makeup to go to school. When I'd started every day on set in hair and makeup, the stylists had always worked to make me look *more* like a kid, not *less* like one. Craving the friendship of kids my age, I quickly tried to get up to speed. By "trying" I mean that I *tried* talking to kids my age. When it came to hair and makeup, I was absolutely clueless. And my mom didn't have time to get my skirt hemmed, so let's just say it was extra, extra long and extra, extra *not cute*. Did I mention I was a tomboy who was a skater poser? I couldn't skate but I so badly wanted to. The fact that all the cool skate shoes were two sizes too big for me did not stop me from buying them and wearing them to school. Yup, long dorky skirt and giant shoes. My look was only getting hotter.

Despite the regular and not-so-regular challenges, I loved being a student in a regular school, especially being a part of the water polo team and running cross-country. My mom, however, wasn't as big of a fan. We'd started to fight, and she blamed the school experience for me acting in ways she thought were disrespectful. After that year my mom pressured me to test out of high school, which is kind of like getting a GED, but I would get it before all the other kids even graduated. You drill down at home to learn as much as you can to pass the test. I would have loved to stay in school, but I did what my mom told me to do.

At the same time I was trying to be super regular, I was getting recognized in public. One weekend my mom and I were at Wango Tango, a daylong concert put on by LA radio station KIIS FM. Because my stomach was feeling messed up, I told her I was going to the bathroom and headed in that direction. Pushing my way through the crowd, I noticed that this girl, who was about twelve, was trailing me. I guessed she had to go, too, because she followed me into the bathroom. But instead of using the facilities, I saw her feet waiting outside the door of my stall.

Fer real?

Then she stuck a KIIS FM program of events under the door.

"Can you sign this?" she asked sweetly.

Are you kidding me right now?

Fifteen-year-old Alexa was a people pleaser, and so without using the toilet, I left my stall and gave her an autograph. I still had to go but didn't want her hovering again, and so I left the bathroom and she followed me out.

"Can we get a picture?" she asked.

"Umm . . ." I paused, still feeling stunned. "Sure."

After smiling for a selfie with this girl who had no boundaries, I said goodbye and told my mom what had happened. And she was livid! It's probably good that girl had gone on her way, because my mom, who got real mama bear about it, was not having it.

But my relationship with my mom continued to be strained. In her eyes, I couldn't do anything right. In my eyes, she couldn't. She was frustrated with me. I was frustrated with her. Because she was so strict, I felt I had to hide things from her, like the still secret on-and-off phone relationship with Nick. There was also the loneliness I was feeling, springing from my confusion about why other girls had it so together and I didn't. *What am I doing wrong?*

I was hungry to have friends. I'd missed the opportunity to have a consistent group of friends as I might have had if I'd attended school longer. Truthfully, I didn't know how to have strong female friendships. I had Sabrina, but she lived over an hour away, so we didn't see each other often, only once every year or so.

Around this time I was cast in the movie *Sleepover*. And you know what they say about art imitating life? Filming *Sleepover* felt a little like that. It was about a friend group of loser girls ignoring parents' rules to sneak out one night to compete with their popular mean girl rivals. And while that wasn't exactly my story, I was facing all the same issues other girls my age were facing.

On the inside I felt like the loser my character Julie embodied. And even on set I clicked more with the girls playing losers like me than the ones playing the popular girls! Looking back, I can see now that I was that insecure girl who tried too hard. I wanted to hang out with all these girls and feel cool, but I was in that natural phase of adolescent life where I was painfully self-conscious. That's what felt so different from being on the *Spy Kids* set—when I was with a group of other kids who were also actors, I was blissfully unaware of myself. But outside of that group, I was second-guessing everything I said, what I thought was cool, and how loud my laugh was. *Did I laugh too hard at that joke?* Regular. Teenage. Girl. Stuff.

When I started *Sleepover*, I still wasn't particularly aware of my body. I knew it could run and jump and throw and dance, and that was enough for me. But I had no real understanding of puberty, the changes and rapid growth of a teenager's body, or the impact certain foods could have on how my body looked from day to day. A few months into filming *Sleepover*, the producers contacted my agents about my weight. Specifically, they were concerned because it was fluctuating. I don't mean they saw me losing weight and were concerned for my health. I mean that they were seeing me looking one way, and then the next day I might appear heavier or bloated. Knowing nothing about health and nutrition, or puberty, or portion control, I'd chow down on mini Snickers at the craft services table, or the mac and cheese at catering, and the next day I'd look super puffy on set. To be fair, they did need to be concerned with continuity within the movie. Seeing an actress looking heavy in one scene and skinny in the next would distract viewers. I get it. But I still wish it would have been handled differently.

The producers called my agents. The agents called my mom. My mom confronted me.

My mom had never hidden her opinions about my weight or appearance. I grew up in a pretty blunt household, but now she had the pressure of the studio behind her. Not knowing what to do during what she thought was a weight-gain season, she gave me diet pills. I wasn't hungry when I took them, but they left me feeling shaky and nauseated. I hated them, but I was a people pleaser, and so I swallowed them and kept working.

Because I felt lonely with no friends, food had become my comfort. And with the other insecurities I was facing, finding solace in food helped to soothe my feelings. Until I was twelve our family had a Colombian nanny named Edda. Because Edda spoke only Spanish, and because my Colombian aunt and abuelita lived with us off and on, I spoke mainly Spanish until I was six or seven. Edda cooked amazing Colombian food for us, like *caldo con pollo* and *carne asada*. In my earliest years Edda had been like a mom to me, and food was one of the ways I received her care.

After Edda, I continued to find comfort in food, but my go-to became any cake batter in the cupboard. I didn't choose cake batter because it was something I particularly *loved*, but because others usually didn't notice if it went missing. If there was a box of cake batter in the house, I'd even go so far as to pull out the plastic bag of dry batter mix and replace the cardboard box in the pantry, as if it were full. Then I'd sneak the batter up to my room, mix it with water, and eat it. Clearly the beginning of a food issue here. When my mom finally caught on, she was furious with me, resulting in a spanking and grounding.

Like any good critical preadolescent worth her salt, I recognized—and exposed—the hypocrisy in my mom's rage. I knew she had a drawer in her bedroom filled with a stash of junk food that none of us were allowed to touch—Twix, Milk Duds, malted milk balls, and M&M's. My mom was coveting and hiding comfort food just like me. So when the issue of my weight came up on the set of *Sleepover*, I already knew where she stood.

I admit that a girl's weight is an incredibly sensitive issue, but the reason I know it could have been handled differently is because I'd *seen* it handled differently. Remember my godmother, Amy, who took me to my first audition with Burt Reynolds? Her daughter was in the entertainment industry, too, and when the issue of her weight came up, Amy was a warrior mama about it.

"I'm not dealing with it," she told the producers. "I think she's perfect. So you guys need to figure it out. I'm not going to tell her she's fat because I don't think she's fat. Your standards are unrealistic."

Since Cassidy was a bit older than me when it happened to her, the situations aren't exactly the same. But what I longed for was the voice of that fierce mama bear to say, "I think she's perfect."

What was crazy is that in the *Sleepover* season, Amy was living with me as my caretaker. I knew she loved me, and I adored her. I felt comfortable telling her anything, especially the stuff that is scary to tell your parents. So the awful thing Amy had faced in the business with her own daughter was now unfolding again with me. She was awesome, too, helping me with meal prep and trying to create healthy habits. She worked to find the best diet for me and my body.

My mom had been modeling since her teen years, so staying slim had always been important to her. In her defense, that's the world she came from so that was the world she knew. After scrambling on what to do and not wanting to give up my eating habits, I naturally thought that the best way to keep weight off— especially after I'd been binge eating on batter, or sweets, or mac and cheese—was to start throwing up. A few years earlier I had seen a "movie of the week" where the main character, played by Calista Flockhart, would binge on pizza and soda and then vomit later. It was the first time I'd seen food consumption portrayed in a negative light. And while it didn't mean much to me when I first viewed it, the possibility of purging stuck with me.

I now understand that because the modeling industry is brutally judgmental of women's bodies, my mom had been poisoned just as I was being poisoned by the industry. She'd bought into the lie of beauty benchmarks that determined whether or not a woman was *enough*. Acceptably attractive women were expected to have a gap between their thighs while standing, to demonstrate that they were thin enough. So I'd stare into the mirror, shifting my stance, searching for that holy gap. But because I don't have wide hips, because I'm not naturally curvy in that way, I now know that my thighs will always touch. I needed to know that when I was a teen. Also, when women starve or overwork their bodies—due to abuse, or sport, or appearance, or other reasons—they stop menstruating. So my mom insisted that the fact that I continued to get my period meant that I was still overweight—because that is what she was told. And, naturally, I believed her.

Because I was able to talk to Amy about anything, I confided in her that I'd tried purging, vomiting up my food after I ate.

"Oh honey," she begged, "please don't do that."

Amy was a Christian, and she consistently spoke life into me, reminding me that I was loved and precious to God and to my mom and to her. She assured me that the way the producers saw me, and my agents saw me, and my mom saw me wasn't the way God saw me. God looked at me and saw someone beautiful. And that's exactly what she reflected for me every day.

My mom was doing what she thought was best at the time. While it is hard for me looking back on that time (as I am sure it is for my mom), I know she loved me. I think she was worried about me and my future in the industry if I gained weight. And sadly she wasn't wrong about that. It was a time when models and actresses were expected to have a rail-thin figure. Lindsay Lohan and Nicole Richie plastered on the cover of every magazine convinced us all that we weren't nearly skinny enough.

When my mom rejoined us after one of her trips, I shared with her what I'd shared with Amy about vomiting. Her response?

She tried to make light of it.

It sucked.

I was hurt that she didn't care more. Honestly, I told her in the hope that it would alarm her. Almost like I was looking for a reaction. The one I received was just not the reaction I was expecting.

Soon she was making me run around our neighborhood to burn calories while she drove in the car behind me, which felt humiliating in front of all our neighbors. I'll just say it was way less fun than running on the school track team.

I was fifteen and annoyed that people cared so much about how I looked. I gobbled up Amy's kindness and was pissed off at everybody else.

Fast forward six months.

I'd turned sixteen, and I'd started throwing up my food after eating. At first I'd do it on occasion, but when I started losing weight and people started praising my appearance, I ramped up the pace.

"You look amazing!" they'd coo.

And that attention and praise fed me and comforted me in a whole new way.

I was a full-time rider on the binge-and-purge roller coaster, vomiting almost twenty times a day. And of course that habit began to interfere with my relationships. Because I'd always have to make sure I had access to a bathroom in which I could vomit, I'd be leaving events early to get home to throw up.

Remember how I always knew that God was with me? Even in the lowest season of my disordered eating, which I hadn't yet reached, I knew God was with me. I suspected He was disappointed and I begged Him to take away my addictive urges. The dichotomy between the damage I was doing to myself and my longing for God and freedom was stark. I could be reading the Bible, binging on Doritos or Twix, and then set down my Bible and go throw it all back up into the toilet.

"God," I'd pray in desperation, "you know this isn't my heart. Help me!"

I know that from the outside, those who haven't been caught in the sticky web of an eating disorder can find it difficult to understand. I hated what I did. I hated who I was when I was doing it. But the thing that was killing me was also the thing that made me feel better. I was still the same girl I'd always been, who loved God and longed for meaningful friendships, but I had a secret I didn't want anyone to discover.

A few people knew. While I find it almost unfathomable now, when I was a teen, I thought throwing up was normal. When I looked around at other actresses in the industry who stayed slim, I just assumed that they were either bulimic or on drugs (and I reasoned that vomiting was better than being on drugs). If my sister and I would be out at a restaurant and see a slender woman eating a cheeseburger, we'd assume that she'd be purging it later. We didn't even have a category for the possibility that it might remain in her body and get digested for nourishment.

In that dark season, I had no idea that God created our bodies and saw them as holy temples. I didn't yet understand that He created food as a gift to fuel those holy temples. I couldn't conceive of food as something beautiful that brings people together.

Because I wanted to please—parents and agents and producers and directors—I told myself, *This is my job. I have to control my weight.* I felt a responsibility to all the people who were impacted by my appearance.

My disordered eating was at its worst when I was living in New York at eighteen, performing in *Hairspray* on Broadway. I was this young kid, alone in the city, who didn't even yet know how the subway worked. My mom had put me on a strict budget. And although my rent was paid, I had only $200 a week to spend. Not only is eating in New York expensive, but binging more food than is necessary can also get pricey. So food I could afford became my comfort: pasta, ramen, chips.

Dancing nonstop on the show, while purging whatever I ate, I quickly shrunk down to ninety pounds. I was so unused to having anything in my stomach that even drinking water felt uncomfortable. It made my stomach feel too full. When I looked in the mirror, I saw a girl whose thighs touched. I saw a girl who could get skinnier if she tried harder, ate less, purged more.

But my secret wasn't as secret as I thought it was—because the producers on the show saw a tiny young girl who was just skin and bones. So they'd carefully ask, "When is your mom coming to see the show?" They assumed that a mother seeing a frail, malnourished daughter would intervene. Would advocate. Would help me find resources to get healthy. But to me, the mom who'd told me that I was overweight if my thighs touched would likely not.

After *Hairspray* I shot *Repo! The Genetic Opera* in Canada before moving back to California. Having been officially declared an adult by my mom, I had no money and was living on Kaley Cuoco's couch.

While I was at Kaley's, I received a phone call from my friend Sean Covel, whom I met through a friend when I was sixteen. He was producing a movie and wanted to offer me a role. I accepted and we connected again on set in Australia while filming *Broken Hill*. Our friendship started with flirting, and in a minute we were a couple. At the time it didn't bother either of us that I was nineteen and he was thirty-one, but some people shared with me that they were weirded out by it, demanding to know what I was thinking. I was thinking he was a pretty great guy. Sean was charismatic and everybody loved him. He was this six-foot-four-inch South Dakotan man from an incredible family. He produced *Napoleon Dynamite*, if that gives you an inkling about his sense of humor. We got serious fast and began thinking about sharing a future together.

Not long after Sean entered my life, another significant man showed up as well.

After my parents had divorced when I was seven, I began to see my dad less and less. My mom had had enough and finally cut him off. Even though he was living between Florida and California, he didn't make an effort to connect with us when he was nearby. When we'd occasionally talk on the phone, he'd often promise that we'd see him "tomorrow." He said it so often that humming the theme song from *Annie*—"Tomorrow"—actually became our family joke. But as a young child, I didn't understand why I wasn't seeing him. As my mom became more resentful of his absence from his daughters' lives, albeit her choice, so did we. He didn't make an effort and neither did we.

But while I was dating Sean, I was on a shoot in Florida when my dad reached out and said he'd love to see me. I wish I could say I welcomed him with open arms, but the hurt I'd felt over the years that he hadn't pursued a relationship with me had hardened my heart. Reluctant but curious, I agreed to meet him only because he'd gone to the trouble of reaching out and finding me.

We met at an upscale restaurant called NOBU, on the ground floor of the hotel where I was staying during the shoot. The place is so overpriced that I would *never* have chosen it other than for convenience and the opportunity to make a quick getaway if things in this meetup went awry. When I walked into the restaurant and my dad rose from a bench to greet me, I offered a cool, obligatory hug.

This was a man who I really didn't know, and so I wasn't sure yet if I could trust him. My gut told me to protect myself. He shared that he'd been trying to get ahold of us for years, through my mom, unsuccessfully. That seemed plausible. He assumed my sisters and I hated him, which was pretty accurate. What I saw that day, over pricey soup and rice, but couldn't receive was that he was truly sorry for his absence and was hungry to be forgiven. Throughout our dinner I was cool, unable to show him any love.

After we connected, my sisters were intrigued, so they also reconnected with him. In fact, Krizia ended up living with him for a couple of years as a teen, and she received from him some of the care and protectiveness for which I'd always hungered.

Although it would take a bit longer for my cool heart to thaw toward him, my dad consistently continued to pursue me. In the middle of a workday, a few months after we connected, I glanced down at my phone to read a text from him: "I love you. I hope you're doing well."

He was trying.

And soon after, I traveled to Florida for work and planned to reconnect with family there, including my dad's side—my tias and tios, aunts and uncles, as well as my abuelita, Yeya (pronounced JAY-ja). Being surrounded by my Colombian family and enveloped in their unconditional love melted the remaining ice around my heart toward my dad. Because of the years I'd lost with my dad, and because we lived on opposite sides of the country, it had been fifteen years since I'd been with some of his side of the family. And yet the moment I walked through my abuelita's front door, it was as if no time had passed. As we gathered around her table, and as she heaped arroz con pollo and carne asada on my plate, the deep longing in my heart for a home in which I was known and received and embraced was satisfied.

I started working on a show called *Ruby & the Rockits*. Created by former teen heartthrob Shaun Cassidy, it also starred his brother Patrick and half brother David. I'd say that my experience on that show was comparable to working on *Spy Kids*. The cast was tight and really cared about one another. They'd even meet up at Shaun's house to watch new episodes of the show. Because my current boyfriend, Sean Covel, wasn't into that, I usually stayed home with him. Now I kick myself for missing out on those moments.

Working alongside those rock stars—*literally*, watch the

reruns if you haven't seen it—was such a privilege and blessing. It was hilarious to see David and all the brothers fighting and fussing at each other like siblings do. David wanted to be taller, so he'd get frustrated if someone was sitting higher than him. When they made fun of him, it was like we all got to be part of the family jokes. And their mom, Shirley Jones, even played our grandma! They made all of us feel like we were part of the family. Rarely do actors get the opportunity to work on a show with that much heart. Austin Butler was part of the cast and one of my closest friends at the time; he was the first person I talked to about my eating disorder.

After my birthday that year, Sean gave me a promise ring, which is like pre-engagement. And when I was back on the set, the people who knew and loved me took notice.

One day Shaun Cassidy and our producer, Marsh McCall, invited me in to their office.

"So," Shaun asked, "what's the deal with that ring?"

"Umm . . ." I offered, feeling more weird than excited. "It's not that we're engaged, but we'll probably get engaged."

I saw concern on their faces.

I remember Shaun saying how much they cared about me and then urging me to give a lot of thought to getting married so young.

Though gentle, and measured, his message was loud and clear.

"We're not saying you shouldn't get married," Marsh added, "but think about it. You're so young."

Although they were hard words to hear, I thought it took *big love* for them to say them. I thought it was brave and kind, and their care has remained with me.

I wish I'd been able to spend more quality time with the rest of the cast and crew, but my eating disorder also took me away from that special group of people. I know I missed out on what I could have enjoyed with them, and I've always wanted to apologize to Shaun and Marsh for not being fully present during that time. Today Marsh has passed, and when I am face-to-face with Shaun again, this is the conversation we'll have.

Several months after talking with Shaun and Marsh, after Sean and I were officially engaged, someone he knew who works with people who have eating disorders pulled him aside to share her concerns about what she'd noticed in my behaviors. He heard her out and confronted me. My biggest fear, that someone would find out, was being realized. But I still wasn't willing to admit it.

"I can't believe you think I have an eating disorder," I sobbed.

After I'd effectively gaslighted him, making him seem like the bad guy, he backed off. "Okay," he apologized, "I'm sorry."

Two months before the wedding, I got a text from my mom announcing that she, Krizia, and my stepdad, Eric, were on their way over to the house Sean and I shared. Together they'd decided that Sean shouldn't marry me without knowing about my eating disorder, and they were going to tell him.

I was in a sound studio recording the audiobook for *Broken Hill* when I got the text, and it terrified me. I looked at my watch and knew I couldn't beat them to my house. In shock, my mind raced to figure out how I could get ahead of them.

All I could do was text Sean: "My family's coming over . . . There's something you should know . . ." Everything I'd so vehemently denied to his face came pouring out.

I missed the summit, but Sean told me what happened. As

they laid it all out on the table, he listened well. He was respectful of them and protective of me.

"Why are you guys coming in now to say this?" he asked them. He understood the seriousness of what we were facing and wished he'd known sooner. Not only was he learning that the person he loved had this huge problem, but he was also discovering that it had been a secret I'd kept from him.

Driving home that evening, I couldn't imagine what my life would be like if they took away what helped me to cope. I felt like I couldn't go on. Speeding past oncoming cars on the highway, I had the thought, *I could just turn my car, like this, and it would be over.*

I felt desperate once I was no longer in control of my secret. The one thing over which I had control, the one thing no one else could touch, was my body. In a world where I performed for the eyes of producers, and directors, and audiences, my eating was the one thing that remained in my control. The disordered eating that *began* as a way to please all those other eyes had become something I now thought I needed to survive.

That night Sean held me and vowed to support me. Keeping his word, he didn't leave my side for a month. He was smart enough to know that I'd try to get away with whatever I could, and that I couldn't be trusted to tell the truth. During that time I was receiving only the smallest bits of nutrition. I'd been throwing up every meal I ate for five-ish years, and I'd brutalized my body so that it no longer could process food naturally. As a result, when I did make an effort to eat again, my body wasn't able to handle food. So two months after I'd stopped binging and purging, I ended up being hospitalized for ulcers, bloating, and other digestive complications. As I tried to reintroduce foods, I met with doctor after doctor to figure out how to help my body function normally again.

Even with all the facts at his fingertips, in 2010 Sean did marry me, when I was a wee babe at just twenty-one years of age. Sean's good friends from college, Doc Wyatt and Dagen Merrill, got "ordained" online in order to marry us! ("Doc" was actually not a doc; he just earned the nickname for his hair that made him look like a crazy-wild mad scientist.) We celebrated our wedding in South Dakota surrounded by close family and friends. And I had Austin Butler as our ring bearer. (I would have made him a bridesmaid if I could!)

Within a year, though, our marriage became pretty difficult. So Sean and I went to counseling through our church. When that wasn't effective, we sought out another Christian counselor.

While we were struggling in our marriage, Doc came to visit us. We shared with him about my eating disorder and the frustrations we were experiencing. I think I expected him to be *disappointed* in us, but I could see in his face that he was just heartbroken. And in his voice, as he cared for me and cared for Sean, I heard this sweet fatherly tone. What I think the counselors and friends and Doc didn't want to say to us was, "You guys shouldn't be together. There's a big age difference. You're in different worlds."

I was working on a show that filmed in New York and Georgia, called *Royal Pains*, and while Sean and I were struggling, I needed to go film in Georgia. When I left, Sean and I hadn't decided whether we were splitting up. We just knew that what we had wasn't good and wasn't improving.

One evening after we'd finished filming, I curled up in bed with my fresh new paperback copy of *Hunger Games*. Between a pair of crisp, clean hotel sheets, I was transported to another world. And that night, escaping my life for another world felt exhilarating. I remember the surprising thought that suddenly filled my mind: *I haven't felt this much joy in years.*

It was the moment I knew my marriage was over.

Today I wouldn't advise anyone to end a marriage based on the kind of discontent and dissatisfaction Sean and I were dealing with. During that season, though, when I truly considered myself to be a Christian and did seek God, I really didn't understand what it meant to trust in and follow Jesus in a radical and personal way. I've since become convinced that when two people are seeking Him, God can restore the most deeply ruptured relationships between husbands and wives. In fact, I've seen it. When we allow God to lead, healing and redemption are possible. If Sean and I had shared that commitment, our story might have unfolded differently.

The version of religion I was living was pretty basic: I'd decided I was a pretty good person, I talked to God, and sometimes I went to church on Sundays. I had no idea that if walking with God was about being a "good person," we wouldn't need Jesus. I did have a relationship with God, but I didn't know Jesus, and I had even less of an idea who the Holy Spirit was.

When I returned home, and Sean and I agreed that we'd exhausted our options and would not be able to stay married, the first friend I called was Daryl, my "brother" from *Spy Kids*, who has always been there for me. He became my closest friend in that season and walked me through my separation from Sean in the spring of 2012. In the next few months, I filmed in Georgia and New York, and I bounced around a little bit, living with friends and sometimes with my family. I'd go out salsa dancing and drinking with my friends Wil, Jess, and Camila, who then felt like family. We even took a few trips to party in Mexico.

I dated different people. Although Sean had been my first and only sexual partner prior to that season, I became more promiscuous than I'm proud of. And I can't even say that I was doing it because I wanted to do it. That people-pleasing part of me— which kind of *sounds* like a good thing, but really isn't—wielded so much influence on my decisions that I was sleeping with guys I was dating because I didn't want them to feel unliked. Crazy, right? But that's where my head was. I was hurting, and I didn't want to hurt anyone else.

Among the guys I dated were an Olympian, a footy (a hybrid of rugby and soccer) player, a fellow actor, and even a rock star, covered head to toe in tattoos. After the rock star and I broke up, I decided that I didn't want to date anyone in the entertainment industry anymore, because so many of those men had "me, me, me!" personalities.

I vowed: *I'm not going to date an actor. I'm not going to date someone who sings.*

My "no way" list was growing. *But little did I know. . . .*

Back when I was a teenager, I'd met a guy named Andrew through a friend of mine named Brene. Her dad was a pastor, and Andrew served at her dad's church. At Brene's fifteenth birthday party, I'd sat beside Andrew, who was about ten years older than I was. I had no idea he would become such a treasured friend.

Named Abdullah at birth, at the age of three he was getting

shot at as his Muslim family ran across the Afghanistan desert in search of safety. When they landed as refugees in Virginia, and later moved to California, he began going by the name Andrew. As an adolescent he struggled emotionally, and he was rescued from his second suicide attempt by someone who stopped him from jumping off a building. I thank God for that person because of who Andrew has been in my life and the lives of so many others. When Andrew met Jesus at age twenty-eight, he became a radical disciple and joined Bishop Ganther's church, Harvest Christian Center, in Inglewood.

After Sean and I split and I was back in LA, Andrew helped me find a house in Porter Ranch, where I lived with my sister Krizia, not too far from Andrew's house. He would invite us to Bible study on the regular, though with my filming schedule it never seemed to work out.

I have this clear memory of riding a bicycle with a guy I was dating while filming a movie in Austin, Texas, when Andrew gave me a call to remind me that Bible study was on Thursday. I remember a loud guy in the background, who was hanging out with Andrew, shouting "What up!?" His name, Andrew told me, was Carlos, and I needed to meet him sometime.

"Sure, sure," I agreed, basically brushing it off.

A few weeks later, when I was back in town, Krizia and I hopped in my green Range Rover to buy a printer at Best Buy. She was waiting in my car out front when Andrew drove by in the passenger seat of this black Escalade that was blasting Jessie J's "Do It Like a Dude."

"Krizia!" Andrew yelled, seeing my car and recognizing my sister.

The vehicle slowed to a stop.

"Hey, Andrew," Krizia answered, "What you doing?"

"Just hanging with this guy," he answered, pointing to his friend who was sitting low in his Escalade, cap turned sideways, thinking he was all that. "Is Alexa here?"

"She's inside," Krizia answered, pointing to the store. "And I think she's planning on coming to Bible study on Thursday."

"Cool," Andrew answered, "that's awesome."

After they left, I came out of Best Buy and dumped my new printer in my trunk. Slipping into the driver's seat, I received Krizia's report.

"I just saw Andrew," she announced, "cruising with some gangster thug."

Little did I know that guy would one day become *my* gangster thug.

Thursday night, as I was en route to Bible study, I was having trouble finding Andrew's place. After pulling into the wrong gated community, I turned around, and when I hit the spikes guarding the neighborhood's entrance, I heard my tire pop. Pulling over, I start texting and calling Andrew, as well as calling for a tow truck. When he got my messages after Bible study, he drove right over to pick me up. I knew I'd missed Bible study, but he welcomed me to hang out a bit with people at his house.

I wasn't there for long when I got the call that the tow truck had arrived, but I did meet this one talkie talkie guy named Carlos, who made me laugh.

"This is the one I was telling you about," Andrew reminded me. "I don't know if you remember."

I did remember him telling me about some guy he wanted me to meet. Andrew hadn't called him a gangster thug, but it wasn't hard to make the connection to the guy Krizia had described. I wouldn't have described him as gangster thug, though. More like Speedy Gonzales meets Pepé Le Pew.

When Andrew and I were leaving his place, this Carlos dude ran over and shouted in my face, "Oh, shiitake mushrooms!" It was a line from *Spy Kids*. My character, Carmen, says it when she's suddenly face-to-face with her evil doppelganger, and it humorously avoids the curse word.

My thought? *That guy is such a weirdo.*

I guess he thought he was funny. Secretly, though, I loved his outgoing confidence.

Andrew was spending a lot of time with Carlos who, Andrew told me, had just met the Lord and was growing in his faith. And in that hard season in the wake of my divorce, I knew that I was also wanting to spend more time with Andrew. I loved his heart, and I wanted to know more of Jesus. Most important, I was ready to be done with my season of partying and to grow more life-giving relationships.

The week after my flat tire, the week when I'd missed Carlos sharing his testimony, I began attending Bible study for real. Though I'd always known I had that craving for God, my personal relationship with Jesus began at that Bible study. While I'd previously had a Sunday-morning understanding of what it meant to know God, I started diving into God's Word and discovering that there was power in it. And on days other than Sunday.

From the outside, my life at twenty-three looked pretty good. The inside, though, told another story. Stinging in the wake of my divorce, I'd been dating around and partying with friends in ways I never had before. I wasn't doing drugs but I was drinking, and that was not normal for me. I was still battling unhealthy eating habits. I was bouncing around, traveling with friends, without creating roots of my own. And while I continued to adore working as an actress, there was still a deep hunger in my heart for more. More satisfaction. More God. More peace. And for the first time in a long time, reconnecting with Andrew gave me hope that I could have all of it.

CHAPTER 5

THAT WEIRD KID

LOS

I knew that Alexa had recently gone through a divorce, and one of the people she was leaning on in that hard season was Andrew. Just like me.

And when Alexa called Andrew the next week to invite him to a party on Friday night, he asked, "Can I bring Carlos?"

"That *weird* kid?" she clarified. "Sure, okay."

Friday night the three of us went to a party together to promote Alexa's recent movie, *Sin City 2*, at a mansion in Beverly Hills. When Alexa noticed that guys were following her around (and, really, can you blame them?), she asked Andrew if he'd pretend to be her boyfriend.

"They're never going to buy that," he told her. Being a little bit older, I guess he thought he didn't look the part.

Turning to me she asked, "Will you do it?"

Will I do it?

"Sure," I agreed. Because that's the kind of guy I am. "I'll take one for the team."

So for the rest of the evening we walked around hand in hand,

and I really thought I was Mr. Macho. We had an awesome time together. Fun fact: at one point during the night we decided to exchange numbers, and we took photos for each other's contact card on our iPhones. (To this day I still have the same photo as Lex's contact in my phone. It's very special to me.)

After the party Andrew and Alexa stopped by my pink house, and I was super proud to show her around my palace. I took Alexa to the garage to show her my cars: a black Cadillac Escalade and a white Mercedes SL550, with matching white wheels and burgundy interior. I thought it would be impressive.

She turned to me and said, "Why do you need two cars?"

I guess she was not so impressed.

Little did she know that in the near future she would desperately need a vehicle to drive when her 2004 Range Rover was finally laid to rest, and a certain someone would be generous to lend her his second car.

The next day Alexa texted me to ask if I wanted to get some fro yo at Menchie's.

Umm . . . yes, please.

After talking and laughing for three hours at Menchie's, neither of us was ready to go home. So, naturally, we went to a trampoline park. As you do. We caravanned there since we were in two cars.

I remember being on the 405, driving behind Lex, and having these butterflies in my stomach. No lie. In fact I had this burst of emotion come over me, and I spoke out loud, "I will marry that girl!" She didn't know it yet, but I was in love.

When we finished jumping and still weren't ready to say goodbye, we hopped in our cars and onto the 118 to head to the home of a friend from church, who was having a birthday party, since we knew Andrew would be there. We had never been to their house before and, honestly, had no idea which one it was. They all looked the same. And it was dark. We saw one with a red door and a lot of people inside and thought for sure that was it. *Knock, knock.*

"*Happy Birthday!*" we screamed when an older woman in her seventies opened the door.

Lex and I exchanged a look, realizing we'd just shouted at a complete stranger.

"You've got the wrong house," she said kindly. "But we're having a wake for my mother, whose birthday would have been today."

Nothing awkward about that.

"Sorry," we apologized, and got out of there.

We found the right house and spent an hour or so hanging out with everyone. Then we both jumped into my Mercedes convertible, dropped the hard top, blasted the heat, turned up some tunes (The Kooks), and cruised Topanga Canyon heading toward the Santa Monica pier.

At the pier, while we rode the Ferris wheel, played carnival games, and ate sticky blue cotton candy, it felt like something special was happening.

After playing at the pier, I was driving Lex back to her car when my phone rang. The dashboard screen of my car made it really plain that Sam was calling. (But the name Sam might belong to a guy, right?) After I'd connected with Sam (the *girl*) at Bible study the previous week, and she was back from her girls' weekend in Vegas, we'd been texting and she admitted she was interested in talking about getting back together. But suddenly this Alexa girl had captured my attention. I toyed with the idea of not answering, but that felt like it would look too suspicious. Like I was trying to *hide* something. Which I absolutely was.

"Hey, Sam," I said answering the phone, cutting off Bluetooth, trying to sound as nonchalant as if it was a guy I was talking to.

Assuming I was alone, Sam started asking me what was up with us. Nothing awkward about that. As soon as I could, I pulled off the freeway and found a place to park so that I could finish the conversation outside of the car.

The moment I pulled over, Alexa, who now obviously knew I was talking to another girl, said, "I'm getting out."

"No, no," I begged, "you stay in the car and I'll get out."

Jumping out, I stepped away from the car to wrap it up with Sam as quickly as I could. I caught Alexa glancing at me as I desperately tried to wiggle out of the conversation.

When I finally hung up, I hopped back in the car trying to pretend like everything was super normal. The look on Alexa's face told me that we weren't okay.

"You know what," she said, "I don't know what's up with you and whoever, but I'm not cool hanging out with someone who doesn't know his situation. Does she even know I was in the car?"

"Not exactly," I hedged.

"That's not fair to her. I don't even know what you two are, but I'm not comfortable with this," Alexa said, pointing between us. "You need to figure out whatever *that* is."

"Yeah," I agreed, "that's probably a good idea."

The last few miles of our drive were pretty quiet.

As I watched Alexa get safely into her car, I knew I had to end things with Sam, just as they were beginning again.

But could I even help it if I accidentally met a totally awesome girl that I knew I was going to marry?! The hangout that started at one in the afternoon lasted until midnight. (It wasn't a date. You got that, right? #notadate #justfriends)

For the next few days, as I tried to end it with Sam, Alexa and I kept chatting but didn't hang out. When I'd glance at my phone on the set and see her name pop up, my heart felt warm and gooey.

While Alexa and I continued our super-platonic friendship, I wasn't the only one who needed to wrap up loose ends. She'd been dating this footy player—oh yeah, did I forget to mention that?—in Australia and had plans to visit him at Thanksgiving.

At the time, I was a pretty jealous guy, and I was not liking the thought of her in Australia with some huge, burly professional athlete dude. Even though we were "just friends," Lex and I were texting and talking every day. And I had no plans to back off just because she was going to Australia. I really did not want her to go, but because we were still "just friends," I played the "do what makes you happy" card. So off she went. Because the time difference was rough, we switched from text to email and had a nonstop Q&A thing going . . .

"What was your favorite book when you were growing up?"

"What's your favorite candy?"

"When you were ten, what did you want to be when you grew up?"

"What makes you feel nostalgic?"

We got to know each other in deeper ways that we might

have missed if we'd met and fast-tracked straight to dating and physical intimacy.

Even though I didn't totally freak out on Alexa while she was in Australia, I was feeling pretty hurt—and wildly jealous—that she'd chosen to go. But when she returned I sucked it up and carried on. I'm glad I did, because her relationship with footy boy didn't last beyond the trip.

Soon, Andrew and Alexa and I were hanging out every day. Friends started calling us "the trio." We'd do dinners, movies, or hangouts at my place or Andrew's. The three of us really loved spending time together, and Andrew was caring for each of us as we closed up difficult chapters in our lives and began to become more serious about our faith. And more serious about each other.

Alexa and I began hanging out on our own, though we were definitely keeping it in the friend zone. Each Sunday she would pick me up for church, insisting I was no good at driving. (She clearly had no idea what she was talking about.) Then we'd do brunch. Maybe a movie.

One Sunday afternoon after church, I invited her over to the home theater in my house because she hadn't seen *Big Time Rush*, and I wanted her to watch the show. I felt like a kid on Christmas morning as I cued up my favorite episode, called "Big Time Love Song," where I got to dress up like a caveman.

Eager, I glanced sideways to see her reaction. To my disappointment, she didn't seem overly impressed.

She laughed. "Los, you look ridiculous."

Okay, that's not at all what I'd been going for. But, to be fair, I was dressed up as a hairy caveman.

In case there was any doubt about her opinion of me and my career, she weighed in bluntly.

"You're such a dork. You literally play a nerd on a kids' TV show."

Ouch.

I was used to girls stroking my ego, and this did not feel like that. I like to think it was just her way of flirting with me.

While we sat side by side, I gathered my courage and reached for her hand.

I felt her quickly pull away.

Bigger ouch.

I knew we had this great vibe. It was undeniable. So I didn't know why she wouldn't just get on board.

A few days later we were watching some Marvel movie. (I can't remember which one because my mind was in a different place.) I decided I should probably try to kiss her. I was feeling it. Leaning in, I turned my face toward hers.

Without taking her eyes off the screen, Lex barked, "Nope!"

She really just said that?!

Yes, she really said it.

Had I been a mind reader, I would have heard Alexa's internal monologue: *I've already done so many stupid things. I really want to do this one right.* And for Alexa, doing it right meant starting as friends first. She also didn't want to ruin our beautiful friendship trio by making things extra awkward. But c'mon! We had been doing this friend thing for almost six weeks! What felt right to her did *not* feel right to me.

A few days later we were watching *Perfume*, one of Lex's favorite movies. To be honest, it wasn't the most romantic movie, but hey, I'll take what I can get. I shifted on the couch we shared to cuddle up against her. Sort of trying to make it seem real natural.

"*Los!*" she hollered, "*Go!*" She was laughing as she was shoving me back to my side of the couch. The girl was cold.

The next weekend we were back on the same couch, watching the cinematic masterpiece that is *Tropic Thunder*. I was laughing at goofy Ben Stiller when I felt Alexa turn toward me, draw closer, and kiss me.

You know how when cartoon characters kiss for the first time, you see fireworks exploding in the sky behind them? Yeah, this was like that.

It was the beginning of "us."

When we went from being in the friend zone to being a couple, we both kind of *knew* that what we had was real. The week after the kiss, we were sitting in front of the fireplace, talking about everything and nothing, and I knew I wanted to hear how she saw her future.

"Dream home!" I commanded. "Go!"

"Excuse me?" she asked, seeking clarification.

"If money were no object, and you could have your dream home, what would it be like? Talk to me."

Thankfully, she was game.

"Okay," she began, "Nashville. I want a big property with a white fence all the way around it."

I knew she'd loved living on a ranch in Florida when she was young, and a big spacious property reminded her of that.

I egged her on to keep telling me more about this dream home. Then, without thinking, I asked, "Do we want horses?"

Did you hear it? I didn't ask her if *she* wanted horses. I asked if *we* wanted horses. But you know what? It didn't feel weird or awkward to either one of us. And before we knew it, we were creating our dream home together. So yeah, we moved from friend zone to imagining "happily ever after" pretty quickly.

Because I'm one of four boys and Lex is the oldest of six, we both could imagine having a bunch of kids. And we knew we wanted to be young parents, like our own parents had been. Neither one of us had any interest in trying to throw a football to our kid in our sixties or seventies.

Okay . . . it got deep fast, didn't it?

As we began spending all of our free time together, each of us knew that we were feeling the *L* word, but neither of us wanted to take the risk to say it first. I already knew that saying "I love you" didn't come naturally to Alexa. She'd dated this guy she'd worked with on *Spy Kids* on and off for six years, and whenever he'd tell her that he loved her, her answer was simply, "Same here."

Pretty romantic, right? In fact, Lex actually got a tattoo on the back of her neck that said, "Same here." (It's still there.) It was meaningful to them, which I get, but it also kind of signals that someone isn't choking out the harder words: "I love you too."

To be fair, Alexa didn't grow up hearing her parents tell her that they loved her. A lot of her mom's and stepdad's actions signaled that they loved Alexa, but they didn't say it in words. So because I knew that "same here" was what she was able to do, I kept my expectations low.

One afternoon after we'd been hanging out at my place, we got in our separate cars so that I could go to work and Alexa could drive home. Hers was a used green-grey Land Rover that was always breaking down and mine was my white Mercedes.

Heading in the same direction on the freeway, we actually ended up driving side by side.

I was hauling in the center lane of traffic and glanced to my right to notice my girl smiling at me. Not an easy moment to keep my eyes on the road, but I pivoted back forward to stay alive. Because she's irresistible, though, I tipped my head back toward Alexa, to see her making these big pantomime gestures. As she mouthed "I," she pointed to herself. Then, as she appeared to shout "love," she used her left pointer finger to trace the outline of a heart against the driver's side window. Finally she poked her finger in my direction as she mouthed the word "you."

Wide-eyed, I asked myself if what I thought just happened had really just happened.

I was pretty sure it had.

Although I knew I shouldn't text while driving, I couldn't resist texting the woman who loved me a series of GIF heart explosions and the words, "I love you too."

Lex here: What actually followed was Carlos racing to the studio where he proceeded to send me three photos. One of Los pointing at his eye. The next a heart made out of Skittles from his dressing room. And the next was a photo of me. It was super cute, and my heart was exploding.

It was official. We were smitten with each other. When December rolled around we went on a cruise with my family, who were all big cruisers. Lex had never been on a cruise, and she was a little hesitant, but we all had the best time. And on

December 29, 2013, I took her to the bow of the ship and asked her to officially be my girlfriend.

She said yes!

At the time I was working on my fourth season of *Big Time Rush*. I was living in the gorgeous home my dad and I had purchased and renovated. I was dating this amazing girl. And, most importantly, I was growing in my faith. I was active at church and in the choir. I was eating up the Word with other believers at Andrew's Bible study. I was on this Jesus high, enjoying the goodness of God in my life. Life was *really* good.

And then it wasn't.

I'd been living in the house that my dad purchased. What had started out as a sprawling pink monstrosity in need of a lot of TLC had become a custom home that I was proud to have renovated. I'd poured time, love, energy, care, and over $250,000 into it. One day Andrew called me and said he had someone who might want to buy my house.

"It's not for sale, dude," I told him.

"Trust me, Los, this could be really good," he assured me.

Not knowing what I might be getting myself into, I agreed to let him show the house that evening. At six o'clock, two blacked-out Escalades pulled into my driveway. Lex and I watched from the living room window as a large man came out from the passenger door of car number one. He proceeded to car number two and opened the back door. Now, I may be in an American boy band, but I'm still Latino at heart, and my eyes could not believe what I was seeing. The Latin legend himself—Marc Anthony!—had come to look at *my house*. He was interested in *my house*. He was coming inside *my house*. Before I could collect my thoughts, he was at the door with Andrew. I gave him a full tour and before he left he pulled me aside asking for my number.

"Sure!" I answered.

He asked if he could come back at ten with his ex-wife.

"Sure!"

Again, I was talking but not really putting two and two together.

As they drove away Lex turned to me and said, "You know who his ex-wife is right?"

I had no idea. I wasn't thinking straight, because . . . I just gave Marc Anthony my number.

Lex grabbed my hand. "JLo!"

Holy wow! Not only was I about to sell my house to *the* Marc Anthony, but I was going to meet another legend, the one and only Jennifer Lopez.

I turned to Lex. "I gotta go shower."

She laughed.

I mean c'mon! It's JLo! What would you do? Unfortunately she did not end up coming that night. But I was smelling good when I sold my house to Marc Anthony.

Unfortunately, though, two days before closing, a pipe burst.

We all know moving is rough, physically and emotionally. Marc had purchased the house mostly furnished, so I only had to get my personal belongings out. Lex and I rented a U-Haul and moved everything ourselves. We even got it done five days early so we could hire a cleaning crew to come in and make sure the house was perfect for Marc. So we were pretty shocked, driving up to this freshly deep-cleaned house, to see what looked like poop and toilet paper all over the driveway. The pipe that broke was our main line out to the sewer. So yeah. It was exactly what it looked like. The rupture caused $20,000 worth of damage.

If that mess had happened to Alexa, I already knew how she would have handled it. Because she trusted that God was a good provider, she'd never been super concerned about money. If she had it, great. If she didn't have it, she knew God would give her what she needed. When she left home at eighteen without any money, she figured it out. And God did provide what she needed when she needed it.

While it's great that this worked for her, I am wired very differently. You know that stereotype about Latin men being emotionally fiery? Yeah, that was me. When good things happened to me, I would be the most joyful guy you've ever met. I mean, like jumping up and down, doing back-flips happy. But when life gave me lemons? Let's just say I was not making lemonade.

When the underground pipe to my home broke, my life was suddenly in limbo until the tangly mess between me, the city, the real estate agents, the insurance company, and the buyer all got sorted out. (Do I wish it happened three days later, after I'd signed it away? No, Marc, I totally don't, dude. I wouldn't do you like that.)

I didn't yet know what had happened or why. I did understand that it wasn't a situation that could be rectified in time for the house closing. I also knew that it was going to cost big dollars. I had to be on set the following day and didn't know how I'd juggle all the things that needed to happen for me to sell the house.

"Okay, okay," Alexa cooed. "Let's talk about this. Let's pray about this. We're gonna figure this out."

Pray?! She might as well have suggested I set myself on fire. I was so new in my faith, and had been riding so high on life, that I didn't yet have an understanding of the ways God accompanies us through the *difficult* times we face.

Over the weeks that followed, I wrestled with the city water department. It turns out the pipe was four feet from being the city's responsibility.

"Four feet!" I kept repeating to myself. I could not believe that four feet was between me and my happiness. "Why, God?" I moaned.

It's funny, now, to think I let those four feet take all my peace.

My initial surprise that Lex would bring God into the worst thing that had ever happened to me, or would ever happen to me (there's that Latin fire), morphed into a deeper resentment toward the Almighty.

I'd been doing everything right. After I came to know Jesus, I'd stopped cursing (well, I might have slipped up during this incident). I hadn't even meant to stop; it was just the fruit of the new life I'd been given. I wasn't drinking or smoking weed like before. I was building a relationship with Christ and others through church and Bible study. I was sharing with others about my newfound faith. And I was even granted a blessed reprieve from my hunger for sex! If that's not supernatural, I don't know what is. I'd been living my life for God, and this was how God repaid me?

I now know that there's no divine tit-for-tat math where God rewards us for being good. But because I believed that my life belonged to God, I couldn't simply wrap my mind around the fact that God had allowed something so awful to happen to me.

One night when Lex and Andrew were hanging out, and they were once again listening to my woes, I put it all on the table. "I am so over this. I think I'm done with God," I announced.

Alexa's eyes grew wide as she looked at me as if I had three heads. "Los," she gently answered, "that's not how it works. It's not like God makes bad things happen to you. That's not who He is."

Andrew underscored, "She's right, man."

Now they're ganging up on me?

I challenged, "It sure seems that way, though, doesn't it?" I had no ability to step outside of myself to see my situation from another perspective. All I could see, and all I cared about, was how I was affected.

I continued to rant, "He's like that old man behind the curtain, in *The Wizard of Oz*, who's pulling levers and making stuff happen. What kind of God is that?"

"It's actually not quite like that." Andrew tried to interject sanity into the conversation in the midst of my petulant rant. This man—whose family had obviously endured a lot more suffering than a busted water pipe—mentioned several people in the Bible who faced challenges with God's help.

"Yeah, whatever," I barked. "That's great for them, but how is God helping me?"

Later that week, after we'd both had long days on set, Lex and I talked on the phone about the only thing I talked about in that season. She'd been so patient with me, so calming, so wise. She'd tried kindness. She'd attempted reason. She'd offered prayer. But I could tell she was losing patience. Emotionally unglued, I was yelling and cursing about my problems.

"I'm done with this!" I announced dramatically. I kept ranting. "You want to tell me that God has a plan when all this crap happens to me? No way!" (To be completely honest, I used much worse language than this, but I don't want to repeat it here.)

She took a breath to get a word in, but my mad monologue was not slowing down.

"You want to sit here and tell me God has a plan for my life? There's no way when all this crap happens. There's no way that God's real if He lets all this junk happen. I'm done with God."

If this was how God treated His family, I was out.

While Lex had been pretty patient with me as I moved through the stages of shock and anger, I'd pushed her to the edge. And now she was the one who was done.

She interrupted my angry loop to say her piece. "If you're done with God," she announced, "I'm done with you."

The hard words quickly sobered me up.

What?

No way.

She can't be serious.

Her voice, though, told me she was.

"I can't be in a relationship with someone who's going to bail on God when things get rough. So why don't you think about what you want."

My world had suddenly come undone.

While my logic seemed completely reasonable to me, Lex's growing commitment to God meant much more to her than our relationship did. Now not only was God screwing me financially, but I was about to lose Alexa.

Really, God? Now you're going to take her from me? What looked like anger on the outside was really fear. I was afraid of losing her, and I was afraid to be alone.

Over the following week I continued to dig in my heels, growing more and more furious with God. And unfortunately Alexa was bearing the brunt of my rage. She was a little freaked out by how crazy I was being.

At the time, I was blind. I'd been busy doing what I thought God wanted so that I could get what I wanted. I couldn't see it at the time, but I think it's how a lot of Christians operate. We mistakenly think that if we do the right stuff, God owes us His blessings. And I was no longer enjoying the blessings. Although it's nowhere in the Bible, this bad logic is what I'd silently believed. To my mind, abandoning my faith was the only option I could see. I was so microfocused on the *wrong* that had been done to me that I wasn't willing to look up to see the face of the God who knew me, loved me, and was with me.

Alexa and I took a beat to decide if or how we wanted to move forward. And poor Andrew had to support us both. When Alexa confided in Andrew that she was done with me, he tried to talk her off the ledge, begging her to work it out with me. And as he cared for me, he exposed that man-behind-the-curtain caricature of God I'd created, helping me begin to see a slightly bigger and fuller picture of who God was in my life and in the world.

The house closing was delayed a week. My insurance fixed the pipe, and an error in their accounting ended up bringing the cost down to only $1,000 out of pocket. Man. Those four feet had rocked my world. Completely. And God actually had me the whole time. But I was wrapped in wanting to control the chaos instead of taking a moment to sit still and ask Him what I needed to do.

As my eyes were slowly opened, I prayed that Alexa would stick with me.

CHAPTER 6

A WHIRLWIND ROMANCE

LEX

Something's wrong with Cruz."

While I was on the set of *The Remaining* in Wilmington, North Carolina, Makenzie called me to tell me that while my mom had been on vacation in Saint Thomas with our younger siblings, our little brother Cruz, who was three, had passed out and slipped into a coma. After a couple of days of testing with no answers, he was medically evacuated from the islands to New York City. Several days later, after endless tests, doctors determined that he had two types of Stage IV cancer.

Carlos and I had been navigating our relationship and growing together. When he finally manned up about his house debacle, I told him I was willing to give us another chance. We were working on our different projects when I heard about Cruz, and as soon as *Big Time Rush* finished shooting Friday night, he hopped a red-eye to come support me in Wilmington. I needed him more than I realized.

When I finally got through to my mom, I asked her when Cruz's father, my stepdad Eric, was coming.

"He doesn't know," she answered coolly.

"What?!" I said, louder than I intended. "Cruz is his *son*. He can't not know."

Unmoved, my mom answered, "This is my kid."

I knew their relationship had been strained since they'd separated before Cruz was born, but I couldn't wrap my mind around what my mom was saying. "Mom, you *have* to tell him. That's his baby!"

"Absolutely not," she said.

I burned inside. Not only did Eric deserve to know his son could die, but this precious three-year-old boy deserved to have all the love and support he could. Furious, I ended our call, knowing exactly what I had to do. I dialed Eric's number and he picked up on the second ring.

"Hey, Lex," he chimed, "good to hear from you."

"Eric," I said, cutting to the chase, "Gina doesn't want to tell you, but you need to know what's going on with Cruz."

As I shared everything I knew about what had happened—Cruz passing out on the island, emergency workers being unable to revive him, doctors searching for answers—I *knew* my mom would be furious. I didn't want to deal with her anger, but there was too much at stake for Eric not to know.

The moment I'd dialed Eric's number, I had—in my mom's eyes—chosen him over her. I knew there would be consequences for my betrayal, but I was willing to face them for Cruz's sake.

Fifteen minutes later, when I saw my mom's number pop up on caller ID, I knew that she'd spoken to Eric and was calling to lay into me. Gathering my courage, I picked up.

During the hurricane of rage coming through the phone, I couldn't get a single word in.

After she'd said her piece, before hanging up, she announced, "You're not my child anymore."

Though I wasn't surprised by her reaction, I felt like I'd been hit by one of North Carolina's coastal hurricanes. And while I understood that people who've been hurt, as I knew my mom had, often hurt other people to release their own pain, the words tore into my heart.

When Carlos arrived a few hours later, he found me curled up on the couch of the little apartment where I was living. Cradling me in his arms as I wept, he let me release the new hurts and old ones I'd been carrying. He was becoming my rock, and when I returned to Los Angeles after finishing *The Remaining*, he and I were on a new level of love and support for each other.

About that time another film I'd acted in was releasing featuring Danny Trejo, who'd been my cool uncle, Machete, from *Spy Kids*. It was even called *Machete* and was directed by Robert Rodriguez, who'd also directed *Spy Kids*. I loved the privilege of working with them both again. The role I played, though, as a sexy, bad-booty assassin, was just a little different from my girl Carmen Cortez. Let's just say that was a season in my life when I had not yet set boundaries on the types of characters I was willing to play.

The night of the movie's premiere at a theater in downtown Los Angeles, Carlos and I both got dressed up for the best red-carpet date night ever—it was also a pivotal evening for us as a couple. While I'd been married to someone in the business, Carlos had never dated someone who really understood the life he lived because none of his prior girlfriends had worked in the industry. That night gave him a whole new way to view our relationship.

My stylists had selected a single-strap floor-length black dress for me. (As much as I would love to give you more details about this beautiful dress, I'm a tomboy at heart and wouldn't even know where to start! Sorry, Wayman and Micah.) I wore pointy heels, my hair was swooped over to one side with curls, and I had diamond-drop earrings dangling from my ears. Though I was not a fan of the closed-toe shoes—I'd almost always rather be wearing flip-flops—I rolled with it. They knew better than I did about the fashion in vogue. Carlos was looking fly in a sharp gray suit with a few buttons undone to show off his sexy chest. After photographers snapped pictures of us together, they wanted some of me alone. So, dutifully, Carlos scooted out of the shots. I loved introducing him to Danny and Robert, and we also chatted with other stars like Sofia Vergara and Mel Gibson.

After the movie and the afterparty, we slid into his Benz to unpack everything. Glad to kick off my heels and throw my earrings in my purse, we dished about how much fun we'd had.

"Babe," he raved, "I'm so proud of you!"

It was kind of like he was just discovering how I paid the bills. To be fair, though, we usually hung out at his place or mine when we weren't working. Or if he was working, I'd chill in his dressing room on set in LA until he was finished with his work day. But he'd never really seen me do my thing, up close.

"Who are you?! You are so cool," he continued.

It's not that he was impressed by the red carpet, or reporters, or other celebrities. He'd done all that before. But his eyes had been opened to the fact that I really did do the same thing as he did, that I totally understood what having a career in acting was like, and it made us feel closer to each other.

Even with that affirming realization, though, I still hadn't been completely transparent with him about my struggles with disordered eating. After Sean had cared for me so vigilantly when my family exposed my secret, I did get a little bit healthier. So when Carlos and I started dating, I wasn't bulimic. But I'd still get triggered. It didn't need to be something huge, like Cruz's illness. More often it would be this tiny little whisper from the Enemy: "Feeling bloated right now? Go ahead and throw up . . ."

Truly, that voice is sinister. I'd wake up in the morning and decide, "I'm not gonna throw up today. I'll eat something healthy, like a salad, and keep it down."

But by late afternoon, the lie had invaded my brain, and I would have thrown up. I didn't understand why I did what I did. The vicious cycle had me in its clutches.

While my second bout of disordered eating wasn't nearly as bad as when I was working on *Hairspray*, what made it worse was that I was keeping it from Carlos. I knew how damaging secrets could be, and I didn't want anything to threaten what we had. Our relationship was so good, it felt unreal. So which was worse? The secret or him finding out about the secret?

I decided to stick with the secret. And yet because I was diving into God's Word and growing in my faith, I became more and more uncomfortable with my own duplicity.

I still can't completely understand what transpired inside me at that time, but I can tell you what happened. I'd always begged God to take away my urges, but daily they'd continue to get the best of me. As I became spiritually stronger, something happened that I'd never experienced before.

One morning as I opened my eyes, I had a deep knowing that

my eating disorder was gone. I just knew. If my eating disorder was a person, I knew that he'd moved out of the house. As I walked down the stairs toward the kitchen, I marveled, *Oh my gosh, it's gone.*

It sounds crazy, right? But I just *knew*. This chain that had kept me bound for seven years was just gone. It had been chopped off and thrown into the pit of hell.

It felt surreal walking into the kitchen without it.

As I poured myself a tall glass of water and cooked some yummy egg whites, the constant feeling that I usually wasn't even aware of was gone.

While I'd love to tell you that I was so full of faith that I knew for certain it wouldn't come back, I wasn't. I couldn't risk that hope. And so I waited.

After a healthy lunch on set that day, I waited to be gripped by the daily, unavoidable urge to binge. But it didn't come. At four o'clock I was still waiting. No urge. I went out with friends from the cast to grab a bite when we finished for the day, expecting that later in the evening I'd be leaning over the toilet.

It never happened.

I wasn't about to trust that having one successful day meant much at all. The following day I waited, with anticipation, for the wily menace that had plagued me for seven years to return.

It didn't.

Even though this was the thing for which I'd prayed for years, begging God to deliver me from, I still couldn't believe that *God had done it*. And I really believe that the gamechanger was that I'd established a regular rhythm of diving into God's Word. I'm not saying that *I did it*. In fact, quite the opposite! In his letter to the church in Ephesus, Paul told the believers about the armor of God that they could wear: the belt of truth, the breastplate of righteousness, feet fitted with the readiness of the gospel, the shield of faith, the helmet of salvation, and the sword of the Spirit (Ephesians 6:14–17). Notice that last one: the sword of the Spirit. That's talking about God's Word. And when I was in my eating disorder, I had no weapon to fight with. I was vulnerable, without any way to defend myself. But being in God's Word and praying God's Word was the protection I needed to finally defeat the enemy that had been killing me. It was my *sword*.

If you're skeptical that it was God who released me from that prison, I get it. But I am certain that God was my helper because I'd been unable to do it on my own for *so long*. If it had been a matter of willpower, believe me: I would have freed myself years earlier. And yet in God's timing, which I don't pretend to understand, He set me free.

For a few weeks I had this feeling like someone—my eating disorder—was going to jump out from behind a building and yell, "Surprise! I'm still here!"

It never happened.

Although I'd been hesitant to share my struggle with Carlos, I couldn't *not* share with him my deliverance. Like Sean, he'd had no idea at all that I'd been plagued with this deep shame. He was so supportive, as I knew he would be, and continued to check in to make sure I was okay.

If you or someone you love is battling an eating disorder, the very best thing you can do is to tell someone who loves you about it. Believe me, I know it feels like death. When I was clutched in the grips of my disordered eating, I was terrified about any-one finding out. And that's exactly how the disorder retains its power. It doesn't *want* you to tell anyone! It knows that when you do, its power begins to dissipate. If you're being bossed around by that sneaky demon today, the best thing you can do is to share your secret with someone who cares. Promise me you will.

After Los sold his pink house to Marc Anthony, we went house hunting together and Los found "our house." It was over an hour from where we were staying near Paramount Studios. I was not at all convinced it was our house, and I made it pretty clear that I did not like the house one bit. But Los believed with every ounce of his being that it was *ours*. So I had a decision to make. Rather than allowing it to become a contentious issue between us, I decided to get on board because I wanted him to know that I trusted him. I was willing to go on the journey with him, even if I wasn't a fan. So I joined him in praying for the house I didn't want. God listened, and we got the house.

Over our first summer together, I was filming *The Hunters* and Carlos was touring with Big Time Rush. Because we'd both been hustling, going in so many directions, missing each other on the road, he'd planned for us to get away on a cruise together and told me to invite whomever I wanted. (Awesome, right?) It would be a chill time at sea for us to reconnect and spend time with friends and family. So we met up in Miami the second week in August to cruise. My sister Makenzie and her best friend, Ashley, were there. My friend Brene, who was the daughter of our pastor, Bishop, came. So did Andrew. My Nana and her sis-ter Jeanie cruised. Carlos's family had always loved cruising, and his brothers Antonio and Javi came with their dad. And a handful of other people from Los's tour also joined us. It was epic.

I really loved seeing Carlos with Kendall, Logan, and James. Kind of like my enduring relationship with Daryl from *Spy Kids*, these guys were like brothers. Brothers who loved each other and also drove each other nuts, 24–7.

At that time my relationship with my mom was still pretty strained from the conflict at the beginning of Cruz's cancer journey. We weren't on speaking terms, so unfortunately she didn't join us. (But I'm delighted to report that today Cruz is healthy and happy!)

To kick off our epic summer vacation, everyone gathered for a group dinner in the private room Carlos had reserved for all of us. He grabbed a glass of champagne to make some toasts and say a few words to everyone who'd shown up to play with us. What I'd learned about that man is that if he has the attention of a whole room, he's going to keep talking. In his exuberance and eloquence, he thanked every person in the room. He thanked Makenzie for being such a great sister to me. He thanked the crew on the ship. He thanked Kendall for being an awesome bandmate. He may as well have thanked the garlic bread on the table for being so delicious. I didn't even care if he didn't get to me, because it had all gone on long enough.

"Alright, babe," I whispered, "let's wind it up. Go ahead and sit down."

Then, with a gleam in his eye, he pivoted toward me and teased, "*And* Alexa . . ."

I guess it was inevitable, but I was sure people were ready to eat. "No, baby," I said quietly, "let's just sit down. Everybody wants to eat."

I resisted, but I knew there was no stopping him once he got on a roll.

Looking out across the room and then tipping his eyes toward mine, he began, "You said to me, if the time ever felt right . . ."

Wait, what? What was happening?

Los smiled at me with a gleam in his eye.

Was he proposing? I was frozen. We'd talked about the future together, and a few weeks earlier he'd even teased, "I guess I have to start figuring out a ring."

"Babe," I had countered, "are you kidding? You know me. Of all people, I am *not* a big jewelry person. If there's a time that feels right to you, you propose. I don't care about a ring."

Despite my resistance, he'd dragged me into Tiffany's the following week to try on a few different rings, reading my reaction to each. After I'd tried on a few traditional rings, he pointed to a setting with a big yellow diamond and asked the clerk to pull it for us. Slipping it on my finger, he looked for my reaction.

"Ugh." I had groaned. "No way." (Okay, maybe I did care a little bit about rings.) "Not a yellow one," I'd coached him.

So as I'm sitting beside him and hear the words, "If the time ever felt right . . ." I knew where he was heading.

"Well," he continued with a huge grin on his face, "lucky for you, I have a ring!"

Our family and friends beamed as he dropped to his knee.

Pulling a small, deep-blue velvet ring box from his pocket and flipping open the lid, he pulled out the ring featuring a yellow diamond that he'd purchased long before we ever set foot in Tiffany's.

Looking at me, he explained, "You're not a regular diamond kind of girl, and I know yellow is your favorite color. Lex, you are like the sunshine."

The room was buzzing with anticipation.

Looking into my eyes, he asked, "Alexa Vega, will you marry me?"

Tears pouring from my eyes, I hugged and kissed him.

"Is that yes?" he asked, wanting to be sure.

"Yes!" I confirmed.

Then he announced it to our guests. "She said yes!"

The room went *wild*. So many of the people we loved were screaming and clapping and celebrating our joy. Only one person in the room that night had been in the dark, and it was me.

Although some of our guests tweeted out their congratulations to us, causing fans to speculate, we didn't officially announce our engagement for another month. Until then, any posts we shared online didn't include my ring. It was nice having something just for us before we announced! By September 2013, though, the world knew that Carlos Pena and Alexa Vega were engaged to be married.

Carlos and I were still young in our faith. We were figuring out what it meant to live a life of following Jesus. After we were engaged and began thinking toward marriage, I found myself thinking more and more about how to best prepare for a Christian marriage.

When we'd moved in together, neither one of us thought much about it. We knew Andrew wasn't thrilled—since he didn't let us share a room when we had to crash at his house for a few weeks before our place was ready—but we didn't give a lot of thought to our sexual relationship. But after our engagement, I started feeling more and more convicted that we shouldn't be sleeping together. When I first brought up the possibility of practicing celibacy until marriage with Carlos, he was not a fan.

"You can't just give it to a person and then take it away!" he argued. "It's mean. It's like giving a kid a piece of cake and then taking it away! You've gotta let the kid finish his cake."

It sounds funny now, but it was a really hard conversation. Honestly, he was pretty upset.

It was a conversation we revisited over the course of a few months, and my stubborn fiancé—who really did want to live a life that honored Christ—slowly softened. We'd both seen our parents' marriages fail, as my first marriage had, and we wanted ours to last. I was crazy about Carlos, and I wanted us to do it right.

It took awhile, but I remained convicted that the gift of sex was meant to be saved for us in marriage. I didn't force Carlos to agree with me. I couldn't. But in time he also sensed that nudge from Holy Spirit and humbly confessed, "We can't do this anymore."

What God was doing inside our hearts turned out to be about more than sex. For the rest of our engagement, Carlos didn't get the sex he wanted. But that's kind of the point, isn't it? *Marriage* isn't about getting what you want. In that most intimate partnership, each partner is called to make sacrifices for the other. So you don't always get all the sex you want. Or you don't always get all the sleep you want. You might not even get the diamond ring you wanted. But what you get, we discovered, can be better than what you thought you wanted.

After Carlos had tricked me into visiting Tiffany's and I bluntly announced how much I did *not* want a yellow diamond ring, he was bummed. Of course. When he'd chosen it, he'd really been thinking about who I was, and he thought I'd love it. And I'm so glad he stayed the course, because from the moment he slipped it on my finger, I absolutely loved it.

As we discussed a ceremony, we decided that we wanted to have an intimate private ceremony before the big shindig with family and friends.

On December 24, 2014, I wore a long, white flowing dress for the private wedding in our home that was being officiated by our pastor, Bishop Ganther. His wife and Andrew were also present for the ceremony. We were married in the prayer room in our home with people we loved and trusted.

And sex? While I wish we hadn't had sex before we were married, I can say that being intimate in marriage, especially a Christian marriage, was a spiritual experience that took our relationship to another level. Enough said.

After our simple service, Los and I said goodbye to Bishop and Lady Audry, and a few days later we headed for the county courthouse to file our paperwork. As we were waiting in line, we still hadn't decided what to do about our last names. We were both known professionally as "Carlos Pena" and "Alexa Vega," and we knew that we *should* probably just keep those names. It certainly would have made our managers happy.

But we really wanted to do something new. We wanted to start fresh together.

"Next!" the clerk called, inviting us forward to file the marriage certificate Bishop had signed.

Handing us a final document to complete, the clerk advised, "Step over here and fill this out. Make sure that your name on here is exactly right."

Stepping toward a nearby counter, we decided to take a chance.

As you already know, we scrapped Carlos Pena and Alexa Vega.

I could have done the traditional thing and taken Los's last name, but that also didn't feel quite like us.

Although "Pena-hyphen-Vega" could have worked for me, or for both of us, we weren't feeling the hyphen.

Whispering in my direction, Carlos suggested, "Let's see if we can get away with PenaVega."

When I nodded my approval, he carefully penned "PenaVega" under "last name." No space. No hyphen. Just a brand new name. Honestly, we didn't even know if what we were doing was legal, but we were about to find out.

Stepping back toward the clerk who held our destiny in his notary stamp, he glanced down quickly, threw down three stamps on all the carbon copies, and sent us on our way.

Here's the thing. Once you have a legal marriage certificate, you can go to the DMV and get a new driver's license. Once you've got the driver's license, you can apply for a passport with your new legal name. And once you've got the passport, you can change the name associated with your social security number.

I still don't know if the guy in the county courthouse had missed his coffee that morning and overlooked our creative license, but what's done is done. And I'm so glad it's done.

When we'd gotten engaged in August, we assumed that we'd be engaged a year like normal people. But when we announced in September, a weekly magazine and a wedding planning company approached us to ask if they could pay for our wedding in exchange for the exclusive rights to the photos.

Heck yeah.

The rub, however, was that it had to be hosted by one of their fancy resort partners. And, oh yeah, it had to happen in *January*. Which was fast. Like . . . *four months* fast.

Although we cared a little bit about what people would think about a brief engagement, we didn't care enough to decline the generous offer we'd received. In fact, it was kind of a no-brainer.

The first weekend in January, all the people we loved gathered at the Riviera Nayarit resort in the beautiful Puerto Vallarta. Over our eight-day stay, we all hung out for a few days at the front end before our beach wedding. Or rather, I should say what was *supposed* to be our beach wedding. The throng of three hundred Mexican fans got too crazy for our seventy-guest event, and we had to move it off the beach and up to the hotel's courtyard. You know what? It worked. I actually think it was better than what we had planned. We got married! And the price was right.

When my marriage to Sean ended, I never imagined meeting someone and marrying so quickly. And you remember that list of guys I wasn't interested in dating? Well, I hadn't stopped at a short list. Not only did I not want to date actors and musicians, but I wasn't particularly interested in Hispanic guys. I didn't have anything against them, but I just hadn't dated any, not to mention maybe I carried some weight of my mom's failed marriage to my Colombian father. The Australian guy I was dating when Carlos and I met had been six foot nine, Sean was six foot four, Nick was also over six feet, and I hadn't imagined I'd ever date a guy who wasn't tall. So the kind of guy I had no intention of dating was absolutely Carlos Pena.

I knew then, and I know now, that Carlos was and is everything I never knew I wanted and needed. When I had no idea that God was caring for me, when I was entirely unaware of His loving-kindness, God always had me in His grip. And *His* list for Alexa Vega was so much better than the one I'd drafted.

I'm convinced that the same is true for you. Whether or not you yet know that you are held in God's love, whether or not you trust Jesus as the One who has a plan for your life, I know that today God has you in His loving care. At each of our special weddings, I got to experience God's goodness toward me in marrying Carlos Pena. God's love for you might not come in the form of a spouse. It may be that God is healing the hurts you endured as a child. Or He inspires and equips you to do that thing you were born to do. Or it might be as simple as God setting you free to love the people around you in ways that only you can. What I know for sure is that the same way God was loving me, and wooing me, and caring for me in ways I couldn't even see, God is loving you.

That doesn't mean things will always work out the way we want them to, and Carlos and I were about to find that out for ourselves.

CHAPTER 7

HOW A HOUSE FROM HELL BROUGHT US CLOSER TO HEAVEN

LOS

When Kendall, Logan, James, and I are on tour, I love what I get to do. Hanging with my boys, performing onstage, meeting fans, and eating amazing food. Best. Job. Ever.

But after giving 100 percent on the road for months, I actually look forward to coming home. And, specifically, I was heading to my *new home* that Lex and I had bought to begin our marriage in. This house was freaking *awesome*. At least I thought so. Lex was never sold on it. In addition to being tucked away on a cliff with an amazing view of the valley, there was a huge pool. I mean *huge*. And guess what? It had a fire pit *in the center*. There was an auto-on switch so if you wanted to turn it on, you had to make the leap from the edge of the pool to the fire pit. Light it. And jump back. But I digress.

When Lex said she didn't like the place, I was bullheaded and pushed forward anyway. And when all the banks said no to my loan application, I wasn't deterred. I'd just put more money down. All I had. I wanted this house.

It looked like there was no way. But once Lex got on board,

we decided to drive by it every day and pray over the house. We bound it in our name. Amen! Even though the house was over an hour from where we were staying, we were determined to show God we wanted this house.

So when a bank finally said yes, we had our house! (It just had almost no furniture, since we were then officially broke.)

So when the fall BTR tour wrapped, and Lex was filming in Canada, I was psyched to return to our beautiful new home. On the last leg of our flight back into LAX, I began imagining cooking in my own kitchen and watching movies in the theater, the only two rooms we could afford to complete in the house. We did not even have a kitchen table. But, hey, we had a theater. Priorities! I was ready to just be *home*. In a space I loved.

So here's the real: if the white Mercedes and the Escalade didn't clue you in, I like nice things. Nice cars. Nice houses. Nice toys. Nice gadgets. I worked hard, I appreciated quality, and so I treated myself to fine things. The new house in West Hills was my dream house. I'd already decked out the home theater to be a chic, comfortable space where Alexa and I could hang out or invite friends over for movies. Because this house didn't need as much TLC as my first house, since it was a newer build, it was already livable and lovable.

After I landed at LAX, a car service drove me home. Every mile we drove from the airport put me one mile closer to the home of my dreams. Truly, anticipating being in this new house, I felt like a kid on Christmas Eve. As the driver pulled away, I turned my shiny new key in the front door lock, disabled the alarm, and dropped my bags by the front door. Flipping on a few lights as I moved through the house, I grabbed some water from the fridge. I knew I needed to decompress after the tour, and I'd been looking forward to watching something epic in our new theater.

Walking down the main hallway to the theater, I opened the door, turned on the lights, and stepped inside.

Squish.

Cool water drenched my socks.

I took another step.

Squish.

Looking down, I saw that the carpet was completely soaked with water throughout the entire room. Checking the walls, I noticed water creeping up the brand-new custom-textured wallpaper. The feet of three long couches were planted in standing water. As I began to process what might have happened in my home while I'd been on the road, my mind went straight to the speaker system that had been installed days earlier.

As I realized the speakers might be damaged, I almost blacked out. Yes, I'm that guy who wants to have amazing sound for my entertainment system. But the dread that crept over me was more serious than not being able to force my friends to listen to the final scene of *End of Watch* in hi-def surround sound. (Trust me. Try it.) Rather, I was bugging out because the Induction Dynamics speaker setup in my theater was a *$40,000* system. But before you judge me, hear me out. The rep for the company had made a deal with me: if my house could be a showroom for them, where people could come and take a listen, he'd give me a deep, deep discount.

Yes, please.

So without pausing to find the source of the water problem,

my body just went into overdrive removing these three massive speakers that were taller and wider than I was, in addition to six surround speakers. Screw by screw, nut by nut, bolt by bolt, I rescued the system.

Does anything about this story sound a little familiar to you? I had not yet recovered from the trauma of the poop pipe in my first home bursting and throwing my life into chaos eight months earlier, and now I'd walked in on another residential water catastrophe.

God, what are you doing to me?!

While Alexa and Andrew had convinced me that God wasn't a cruel puppet master who sent indiscriminate blessings and curses on unsuspecting people, I still didn't understand why I'd been visited once again by the house drama demon.

Although I'd cleaned up my foul language since coming to know Christ, I dropped a few choice words I had left in the vault when I entered that home theater.

My first call was to Andrew.

Second call was to Alexa.

She picked up just before midnight.

"Hey, babe," she cooed, assuming that since I'd just arrived home I'd be in a better mood than I actually was.

"There's a *flood* in the theater room!" I exploded, rushing on to describe walking in and discovering the watery disaster.

"Slow down, Los," she calmly soothed, "tell me what's going on."

I most certainly did not slow down or quiet down or calm down. Whatever was happening in my house had thrown a house-size wrench into my life.

Hours later, when I finally crashed into my own bed, my mind raced. I knew that in a few short hours I needed to begin making an endless series of calls to get the problem fixed and paid for. In the midst of that angry mental monologue, though, I heard Lex's soothing voice, reminding me that it was just *stuff*. And while I knew that was true, it didn't put a dent in the mountain of fury that was growing inside me.

Unlike having, oh let's say . . . a leaky *faucet* from normal wear and tear, I learned that this issue had sprung from a faulty build. And the substandard waterproofing meant that the house needed extensive remediation. And because of the risk of mold, the next morning workers were ripping out carpets, cutting open walls, installing dehumidifiers, and whatever else they had to do in their quest to keep the mold out. Each day the costs mounted, and I began to get more and more upset. Now, if I'd left a faucet running before leaving for tour, I would have owned up to my mistake and eaten the repair costs. I'd have been shocked and disappointed that the costs were so high, but this? The responsibility for this was on the builder. And as much as I wanted to make the repairs and move on, my attorney said that we couldn't fix anything. We needed to leave the guts of my house naked and exposed for further investigation and evidence.

We'd only owned the ill-fated house for *four weeks*, and now phone calls and letters were flying between attorneys and the builder and subcontractors. And we had to keep living our lives. Lex was filming *The Tomorrow People* and I was back auditioning for projects since BTR had ended, though none were coming through. And something new was also being birthed.

About six months earlier, Bishop and Andrew had begun

asking if we'd be willing to host a Bible study in our home. The congregation at Harvest Christian Center was on the older side, and Bishop and Andrew were encouraging Lex and me to welcome younger folks to encounter Christ. Gentle, not pushing, Andrew and Bishop would always say, "When you're ready. When you're ready."

I was never ready.

But a few weeks after the water debacle, they revisited the idea with us. At first I wasn't down for it. I already wasn't a huge fan of having lots of people in my private space, and the under-construction house made that possibility feel even worse. But gentle Alexa, spirited Andrew, and wise Bishop wore me down. I'd love to say that my heart was changed and I suddenly became some altruistic saint, but it's more fair to say that my attitude was along the lines of: "Screw it! I don't care anymore. Whatever. We'll do it." And, thankfully, that was enough for God to do His thing.

Best.

Decision.

Ever.

Although I'd been a little reluctant about opening our home, when I'm in, I'm *all in*.

The first night we hosted Bible study for about a dozen of our friends, I was hooked.

"Lex," I said enthusiastically, after we said goodbye to our last guest, "why didn't we do this sooner?"

Being keenly aware of my long-term resistance, she just rolled her eyes.

The first guests started to invite their friends, and week by week the Bible study grew in numbers. A lot of these were people who wouldn't be comfortable going to a *church* but were willing to come to our living room and talk about the Bible.

As more folks began to show up, I bought four dozen church chairs to set up in our living and dining area. I got a whole sound system with a mixer, mics, speakers. And we delegated the weekly work to various teams of friends. The worship team included two violinists, a guitar player, a piano player, and a guy on the bongo drums. Cooking crew showed up at six every Monday evening to cook dinner, with Lex, for fifty people. Setup team came early, too, to set up chairs and the sound system. Monday nights we'd worship from eight to eight thirty, then pray, and then have some teaching before taking prayer requests and closing in prayer. After wrapping at nine thirty, everyone would eat and hang out, leaving around eleven or twelve. And cleanup crew stayed even later.

A bit before seven, folks would begin rolling in. Flooding our street with parked cars, friends and friends-of-friends would show up to enjoy fellowship, dinner, worship, and Bible study. (Truth be told, Lex's arroz con pollo was why many came. She would make so much that we would send everyone home with food for the week!) Week after week young adults, single and married, White and Brown and Black, who knew and did not yet know Jesus, gathered to receive what God had for us.

Each week Lex and I would prep to lead the Bible study together. We weren't authoritarian leaders who presumed to have all the answers, though. We were more like, "Hey, this is what we learned this week. What are you learning?" And if you know the way Jesus taught crowds, He told stories and He helped audiences know and understand who His Father is. As a teaching duo, I was the storyteller. I wanted to take those who showed up on a journey and make stories from the Bible interesting for them. Did I make stories from the Scriptures funny? Ask around, but I like to think I did. Lex, on the other hand, was the theologian of our team. She did the rigorous study and brought the theological meat to our teaching. Truly, she killed it.

Although people sometimes think the Bible is antiquated and outdated, no one who came to those Bible studies would have said it. Every week Lex and I were discovering how that ancient Word spoke directly into our lives, and others were too. When you set your mind to listening for God's voice in Scripture, it's amazing how it speaks so personally to issues with family members, conflicts at work, and even leaky houses!

Not long after we'd started, a 5.1 earthquake hit Los Angeles, breaking water mains and rocking communities. Though our home had been spared damage from the quake, and everybody in the Bible study had remained physically safe, we knew that many communities were suffering. So all of us gathered out back, taking in this expansive view of the city, and began worshiping God and praying for Him to intercede in the lives of those who'd been affected. I even noticed a few women and men who'd never prayed aloud in our group offered prayers for the people of our city. I remember blasting "Oceans" by Hillsong on my outside speakers. *Loud.* It was amazing that God even chose to use our incredible backyard view to be glorified.

We committed to hosting Bible study one full year, every Monday night. And if Lex and I had to be away for work, someone else would organize and host the group in our home.

That—strangers hosting an event in *my* home—is a testimony to the grace and power of God. Can I get an *amen*?

Week after week friends and strangers gathered in our broken-down home to learn about God and experience His love for them. In the space where we gathered, large wooden pallets had been erected to cover water-damaged walls. It's not the space into which I would have wanted to invite others, but it's what we had, and God used it.

That Bible study totally changed our lives. It provided us with community we didn't even realize we needed, and it fed our spirits and helped us continue to grow in Christ. It was as if God was smiling and whispering, "If you're gonna fight for that dumb house, then I'm gonna do something special in it." That's the God I was coming to know. He took whatever crumbly offerings we gave Him and used them to build His kingdom.

In that first year of our marriage, Lex and I continued to discover how very different we were, and the issues we were facing with our home were our classroom. For years I'd been working hard to make money so that I could buy what I wanted and do what I wanted. But suddenly I felt trapped by the house I'd been so intent on buying. I'd poured everything I'd made over the years from Big Time Rush into that house and had nothing to show for it. My identity was completely wrapped up in it. So when *it* began falling apart, so did I.

While I'd watched my dad and mom find meaning in nice things, and aspired to do the same, Alexa wasn't as attached to the things of the world as I was. From the financial bumps her family faced as she grew up, she'd already learned that money comes and goes. She didn't find comfort in it the way that I did.

Her freedom frustrated the hell out of me. I just couldn't understand it. When we looked at the same house, we saw it completely differently.

I looked at our house and thought, *Booo . . . the walls are rotting.*

Cup half empty.

She looked at our house and thought, *Yay . . . we have a roof over our heads!*

Cup half full.

It was this unpleasant conversation between us that never ended, and in the war against our rotten home, it sometimes felt like we were on opposing sides. Over the months and years, I continued to resist her optimism.

"You're crazy," I'd bark at her.

"It's our money," I'd insist.

"They screwed us," I'd roar.

Gosh, she was patient with me! With her signature compassion, Lex could see that instead of leaning in to God, my heart was closed off. She heard it in my prayers. When I cried out to God demanding to know why this was happening, she understood that my faith was still growing. But instead of judging me, she was patient with me. And I suspect that her overwhelming confidence in God's goodness and provision sustained me in ways I don't even fully understand. Truly, her faith was so solid that she knew herself to be fully covered by God even if we never got the money back on the house. She still trusted entirely in Him and had this peace that God was going to show up and take care of us. Man, I wanted that so badly. But it was hard for me.

I knew that the problems we were facing were the bougie

problems of privileged people. And if you're living paycheck to paycheck, for me to even talk about our problems might make you roll your eyes. I get it. And if that's you, I actually kind of get you more than I ever would have before that moment. Because we were at a point where we were saying to ourselves, "What work can we get this month so that we can pay the mortgage *and* attorney fees?" Every month we were hustling to get some sort of acting work. Anything! We had so many overhead costs that we had to trust God to provide month to month. And although Lex had trusted God in that way before, I never had. Slowly, though, I would begin to listen to the woman who was my voice of reason.

Jumping ahead a bit, here's how our house drama finally unfolded.

Leaky house number two had gotten the best of us. After three years of not being able to fix any of the issues related to that flooding and because of the ongoing lawsuit, we were eager for a change. But we couldn't sell the house, because we'd lose not just the house we thought we'd be living in together but also the money we had invested in it. And I was not going to walk away from all my Big Time Rush money that I'd put into it. Barely getting by each month, we'd been praying. And we prayed until we felt God calling us to Hawaii.

And then, in a leap of faith, while our LA house was still a mess, we decided to spend a wild couple of weeks in Hawaii to test the waters while Alexa's dad and sister watched the house in California.

One Saturday morning I woke up and wandered into the kitchen where Lex was fixing breakfast.

"Babe," she began, as I sat down on a stool at the kitchen

island, "I was praying, and God said He's already paid us back. We got the money we needed. We gotta let the house go."

Three years earlier, those would have been fighting words. I would have blown a gasket over the injustice of it and dug my heels in even deeper. But I was weary. We were spending all our money, and I still couldn't see how we'd ever recoup it. We'd also learned that the builder was willing to buy the house back. I was surprised to even be considering the possibility, but in that moment her words made sense.

I also trusted that she had a direct line to God. Kidding. Not kidding. She'd get up at four in the morning to hole up in the prayer room and spend several hours with God. I won't lie: I hated hearing her leave our cozy bed, grab her Bible, and close the door behind her. A menacing voice that was *not* from God would hiss in my ear, *She's leaving you to go pray*, and I hated it. First I was enraged. And then I was convicted. That's my wife. And it's just one of the ways she makes me better.

As she dished our omelettes onto plates, Lex continued, "Let's stop chasing the money. Let's let it go."

As was so often the case, she was right. I knew she was. And in that moment, I felt a weight that I hadn't even realized I'd been carrying lift off me. I mean, when I became willing to receive and digest her holy logic, I felt lighter than I had in years.

The idol of the beautiful life I'd imagined in my head was being destroyed. Drop by drop, leak by leak. Without Lex, I would have bailed on God. Without God, I would have clung even tighter to the idol that was failing before my eyes. But the fine, fancy things in which I'd found comfort and security hadn't delivered. I let go of the security I found in owning the perfect house. I let go of hoarding the space I would have wanted to preserve as ours by inviting fifty people into our home each week.

And the surprise that I'd discover, that may not be a surprise for you, was that in letting go, I received so much more than I could have imagined.

Monday morning I called our attorney to let him know that we were going to let the builder buy the house back for what we owed the bank. We were basically giving it to him. I mean we were walking away from it all. Everything I put into the house, which was everything I made during BTR: *gone*.

"Are you kidding?" our attorney asked incredulously.

"Not at all," I confirmed, "we're done. We just want to be done."

It was a very pivotal moment for me. When God led us to release the house, it broke the power that material things had over me. I had idolized the cars, the house, the money in the bank. But truly, after that they didn't matter anymore. Do I still like owning nice things? Of course. But they don't own me anymore. And I know myself well enough to know that if all that hadn't happened—the first house, and the second one, and even being persuaded to share my space—I wouldn't have given it all up on my own. I'd still be stuck, in bondage to stuff. I'm convinced that until you let it go, you can't really know that freedom. Because what I gained when I finally let go was more than I could imagine.

I had my amazing wife.

I had confidence in God's provision.

And I had peace that I'd been missing for over three years.

Today I'm so much more confident that what happens—even if I don't understand it—happens for a reason that God understands and has in His care. And I'm content in that. Because I can't always see it in the moment, I'm asking God to teach me to have that kind of vision.

As my grip on money and what it buys loosened, we were also learning what it means to give. Together we became more and more convinced that God owns everything and entrusts us to be faithful stewards of it all. The blessings we receive aren't just for us; they're for all the people God loves. At Harvest Christian Center we were being reminded regularly that God loves a cheerful giver, and together we wanted to be those kinds of givers. And I've seen what that looks like in Lex. Before we were married she learned of a particular someone who had a particular need. And after cheerfully writing them a check for $800, she had five dollars left.

Five.

Dollars.

My woman trusts God with a fierceness that blows me away.

And the week after she wrote the check? She was offered a movie that would more than pay her bills. And there it is.

The day we signed the papers to sell our home back to the builder, we were free. Free for whatever God had next for us.

CHAPTER 8

BETTER TOGETHER

LEX

"Hey, man." I overheard Los answer his phone moments before we lifted off for a film festival in the Cayman Islands. He added, "We're at LAX about to take off, but what's up?"

"Mm-hmm . . ." he nodded, listening to whatever was being said.

Flight attendants paced the aisles, checking to make sure seat-belts were secured.

Turning to me, he flipped his phone to show me that it was his agent who'd called, so I assumed he was being offered a gig.

"Let me talk to Lex," he said, "and I'll call you after this flight."

Hanging up, he began to tell me, "Well this is weird, but they want me to do *Dancing with the Stars*."

I hadn't seen it, but I told him, "My mom loves that show! That's awesome!"

"And," he continued with a grin, "I think they want you too."

My phone rang, and we saw the name of my agent.

"Pick it up! Pick it up!" he coached.

Grabbing the call, I quickly explained, "Hey, on a plane, need to shut off my phone. Is it quick?"

I listened as my agent quickly downloaded the deets about the opportunity and confirmed that they were interested in Carlos too. While we were dating, Los and I had filmed one movie together, *Spare Parts*, with George Lopez and Marisa Tomei, and it had been so fun to work together, especially since it was Carlos's first feature film.

"*Dancing with the Stars*?" Carlos asked hopefully.

"Yup," I confirmed. "*Dancing with the Stars*. And she said that if we do it, we'll be the first married couple ever."

"Wait," he clarified. "The first ever?"

"Yeah," I said excitedly, "I think so!"

We had been discussing how we could do more projects together, and this one, which we hadn't even gone looking for, seemed to have just landed in our seatbelt-buckled laps.

The voice of a flight attendant droned on the PA system, "Please turn off all personal electronic devices, including laptops and cell phones. . . ."

Shutting off our phones, we dished about the possibility.

"James did it a few seasons ago," Los reported, "and I think he had fun. But I heard it was a *ton* of work."

As we ascended over the Pacific Ocean during takeoff, we tried to decide whether it was a gig that had our names on it. Even though we'd been noodling about how we could do some movies together, the thought of this show had never crossed our minds.

"Babe," Los suggested, "I think we should do it. I actually think we'd kill."

"I think you're right," I agreed eagerly.

I knew we'd have a blast on the show, and even thought that we each might be competitive contestants, but there was another reason we were both eager to sign on. Although our first year of marriage had been tricky, with a few professional challenges for Los in particular, we loved being married. But as we looked around at our friends, and even peers who were as much as a decade older than us, we just didn't see many who were interested in getting married and having kids. Instead, they'd joke around, making marriage seem like a death sentence. But we'd found it to be just the opposite. For us, marriage was that place where each of us was becoming the best version of ourselves, with the help of God and each other, and we welcomed the opportunity to witness to the *goodness* of the gift God offers by sharing our real lives with viewers—and readers.

You'd think that anyone would jump at the chance to be on the popular reality show, but the truth is that for us to say yes, it did need to be both of us. If they hadn't called Los, I would have politely declined. And if they hadn't asked me, he would also have said no. But dancing on the show *at the same time* felt really right to us. And even though we'd done *Spare Parts*, playing a boyfriend and girlfriend in high school, this was the first time we'd be introduced to the world as Lex and Los. We were so *in*.

The first day we showed up for rehearsals, we were totally pumped. Los was matched with the talented Witney Carson, and my partner was the creative Mark Ballas. By that time we'd watched a few episodes, talked to the show's biggest fan—who is *my mom*—and gotten the scoop from James. From watching the show, we had seen the sexual tension between the celebrities and their professional partners. It didn't seem to matter if either one was single or married. That tension captivates viewers and creates exciting television. We weren't too concerned about it.

What we hadn't anticipated was the number of hours we'd be working and how little time we'd actually have to spend together. We'd gotten kind of spoiled, working on *Spare Parts* and having our downtime at home, and we were used to being pretty connected throughout the day. And while the steps came pretty easy for Los, I found that learning all the new choreography took a lot of my focus and attention.

I'd always loved dancing, and as a kid I'd been pretty good. I'd grown up taking hip-hop for six years, and there was all that off-set break-dancing on the *Spy Kids 2* set. At age twenty I had danced on Broadway as Penny Pingleton in *Hairspray*. But at twenty-seven, I'd lost a little confidence in my skills. Los, however, who'd been learning choreography for years for Big Time Rush, had all the confidence in the world.

I think both of us had imagined that the two of us, and Mark and Witney, would be hanging out all day, rehearsing in the same room. On day one we realized that was absolutely *not* the case. Each pair of dancers had their own practice room, and that's where we hunkered down to work long hours every day. It was this weird tension of living in two worlds: in one world I was married to Los and wanted to take breaks to connect with him; and in the other world all my attention needed to be focused on the work Mark and I were doing together. While I don't think that having a spouse on set distracted us from the work we were there to do, our marriage probably impacted the vibe we had with our dance partners. Even though rehearsals are intense for everybody who does the show, we had to make sure that our partners weren't the only people in our lives.

I did experience a unique convergence of those relationships.

At that time Los was still a husband who got jealous and could act a little bit needy. And I know that the fact that it took me more time to learn the choreography, keeping me in our practice room for more hours, was frustrating for him. The effort I was putting in to prep for the show was more than the effort it took for him. We both had to figure out a new rhythm.

Truly, Los made it seem effortless. That man's got talent. His mom has videos of him doing these pirouettes as a nine-year-old. I mean, what kid even does that? And on top of his natural talent, he'd studied dance at the Boston Conservatory. So the dances Witney was teaching him came easy for him.

Not so much for me. Daily I started to feel the uncomfortable pull of having to choose between Los and Mark—crazy, I know— and although I'll always put my husband first, I knew that doing so would actually hurt *me* in the competition. So that particular dynamic was one we had to figure out together. Let's just say that season was extra hard on me. Physically and emotionally.

The first dance each of us did on live national TV was the jive. I danced to "Whistle (While You Work It)," and Los danced to James Brown's "I Got You." After you finish this book, please find his dance on YouTube under "DWTS Season 21." I mean really *watch him*. He's not thinking about choreography. He's not worried about steps. He just looks like he's doing the thing that he was *born* to do. I was so proud of him. I mean, I had fun, too, but I was thinking about the choreography the whole time. Not Los. It's like the dance was inside him and it just *moved him*.

The producers had us doing the same style of dance to heighten a sense of competition between us. The irony is that I'm not very competitive, but what we discovered during the show that week is that Carlos is *very* competitive. (Too bad he hadn't been on the show during the same season his BTR buddy James was!) I don't mean he was competitive in an ugly way. Like, it wasn't that he wanted me to lose. He just wanted to do *better* than I did. That's a little more gracious, isn't it?

I danced my favorite dance of the whole season during the second week. I loved dancing salsa with Mark, both because I love Spanish music and I loved embracing my Colombian heritage. The best memories I have of my family are being together as a family eating sancocho cooked outside in this huge hanging cauldron over a fire pit. During the five hours that the dish took to cook, everybody would be outside singing and dancing on our ranch in Ocala, Florida. Salsa is in my blood. So when Mark and I got to salsa dance the second week to "Que Es Lo Que Quiere Esa Nena" from C+C Music Factory, I was thrilled. I probably had the most fun with that dance on the show since it came most naturally to me. Since I was already familiar with salsa, I was able to be free because I wasn't overanalyzing it like I was doing with the *new* dances I was learning. I was able to just cut loose and enjoy without overthinking it because that was my *jam*.

On week three I danced jazz to the theme song from one of Carlos's favorite shows, *Breaking Bad*. Mark and I were costumed in full-length safety suits to look like chemists in a meth lab. As we walked over to the judges' table, I thought we'd nailed it, but I wasn't sure. For the first two weeks I'd been disappointed to get scores that were only 7s and 8s. But on week three, not only did I get my *first 9*, I got *all 9s*! I was so psyched.

That week the guest judge was Alfonso Ribeiro, aka Carlton on *The Fresh Prince of Bel-Air*. (Pretty cool we had a judge who'd coined his own signature dance move!) He'd won *DWTS* in season nineteen, and now he was sitting at the judges' table. Alfonso and I had known each other for years, so it felt comforting to see a familiar face. But after he praised the job Mark and I had done on the dance floor, the comments he offered next were hard to hear.

"What I want you to remember," he said, looking in my eyes, "is that you two can *win*." Then he continued, to emphasize, "You and Carlos can *not*." Pointing to Mark, he emphasized, "*This* is your relationship in this ballroom. And remember that going forward."

Since I was already busy trying to juggle my priorities with Mark and Los, Alfonso's pronouncement was hard to hear. Because I was looking at the judges, I couldn't see Carlos's reaction, but I knew that neither one of us welcomed the hard words.

By the time Alfonso wrapped up his remarks by insisting, "You can win!" I was already distracted thinking about what my husband was hearing and by my own feelings. I naturally assumed Alfonso was there as my friend, but he was there in business mode. I wanted him to speak to me as a friend who cared about my marriage, but as a previous winner, he was about the business of coaching me how to win the contest. He was able to separate friendship and business. I wasn't. And it hurt.

Los had already danced that evening, earning 7s and 8s dancing jazz to the theme song of *The Golden Girls*. (That's right, we danced to the opening sounds of two very different shows.) He was costumed like an old man, with grey hair and an old striped sweater. Following Alfonso's remarks, host Tom Bergeron pointed to Carlos and remarked, "Even grampa is applauding up there." When the camera cut to Los, he was moving his hands back and forth, but his face showed *me* how disappointed he was by Alfonso's comments. (My man can't hide his emotions even when he tries.) That observation stung because there was also an element of it that we knew was true. I would have the best chance of winning if I was distracted from Carlos and focused only on my dancing and my partner.

The fact that we were both called out like that, on live TV, made me mad. And I was particularly mad at Alfonso for throwing me under the bus like that. I absolutely love Al and I have since moved on, but I was pretty upset at the time. Los and I *chose to* prioritize each other, and no competition was going to change that.

What was awesome is that our fans came out and had our backs. We'd been transparent throughout the show about our commitment to marriage and our love for each other. After week three, fan mail started pouring in to the studio thanking us for representing marriage well. Young people were excited to see a marriage that looked like something they could want. They saw how we loved each other and they cheered us on. A few older couples even told us that it reignited their marriages! The surprise for all of us was that instead of turning on us or second-guessing our commitment to the show, they rallied behind us. That certainly wasn't our intention, but we had decided that however the show unfolded, we would choose our marriage.

Both Los and I now point to that season, and maybe even that show, as the beginning of "Lex and Los." The world was seeing us as the strong team that we were. We were one, and we were proud to be one.

When I speak transparently about the value Carlos and I

place on marriage, it's not lost on me that I'm doing it as a woman who's been divorced. My hope, though, is that rather than that diminishing my message, it might bolster it. The media and entertainment industry have succeeded at painting a dull picture of marriage, making it hard to find on-screen couples—playing their paid roles or their real-life ones!—who model a vibrant, thriving, fruitful marriage. More often, the institution of marriage is viewed as death-dealing rather than life-giving. But for Carlos and me, marriage has made us stronger and better and more unstoppable than we were alone. It's helped us to grow and mature in ways we wouldn't have if we'd stayed single. What I've experienced in marriage isn't the ball-and-chain weight many have ascribed to marriage; it's actually been a *freedom* from that weight.

Dating was fun, but it was *weighty* fun. You don't know where it's going. You don't know if you're going to break up. Anyone who's hustled at the dating game—meeting people at bars, or parties, or at the park, or on dating apps—has described how exhausting it can be. How heavy it can be. The solid stability of a Christian marriage is freedom from that heavy, exhausting hustle. The commitment between you and your spouse frees you both to soar, becoming your best self, and it also frees you to dig into the hard places together. Believe me, there have been a number of bumps during our marriage when, if we'd not been married, we would have broken up. But the security of our God-focused marriage gave us this strong foundation to work through the bumps and land stronger on the other side.

In fact, Los was able to share more of our focus on God during the fourth week of the show. In the package the show filmed before the live show aired, Los had the opportunity to share about his faith. He'd told me he wanted to do it, and when I saw the show, I was so proud of him.

"My most memorable year was 2012," he explained. "My band, Big Time Rush, was at the peak of our success." He then shared that difficult season when he came home from tour with Big Time Rush and hit rock bottom after breaking up with Sam: holing up at home, suffering from depression, seeing no one, and smoking weed. The show interviewed both our pastor, Bishop, and also Andrew, who'd been the person to invite Los to church.

"I walked into the church," Los shared, "and I knew that I was supposed to be there."

One of the first songs he heard there was "Amazing Grace."

Los explained, "From that Sunday to the next Sunday, my life changed forever. On Thursday I got invited to a Bible study. And at that Bible study I met my wife."

That week Los chose to dance the waltz to "Amazing Grace." Hearing his story, Witney used pieces from Carlos's spiritual journey to choreograph their dance, coaching him as they rehearsed, "You found your faith, you found Alexa, you're not lost anymore."

Los and I were so thankful that God could use that crazy reality show to share Los's testimony with the world.

Bawling, Los explained, "It's so crazy to me that in one week, my life changed forever."

As much fun as the show was, and as awesome as it was that it paid the bills, I suspect the most important thing that came out of it was that viewers were able to hear Carlos speak about how faith in God had changed his life. I was beyond proud of him.

On one level, the show's dramatic tension makes the best experience for viewers. But at another level, eating and sleeping and breathing the show day in and day out means that—for that season of time—it really is the most important thing in your life. It just is. So as competitors, we get sucked into that real-life drama.

For example, the seventh week, when I was doing the paso doble with Mark, my foot slipped at the end of the dance. Afterward, I could tell that he was *really* bummed about it. All I wanted was to do my best so that Mark and I could move forward in the competition, and I hated that I'd let him down.

You really give it your all, and when it doesn't work out the way you want it to, it's beyond frustrating. I still had a lot of people-pleasing qualities, as well as a need to keep the peace while performing on *DWTS*. So when I messed up or caused Mark to be let down, it took a toll on me. In a cycle of trying to keep Los and Mark happy—while remembering difficult dance moves!—I was attending to everyone else's feelings but my own.

The eighth week of the show, during partner switch-up week, I danced the tango to Pet Shop Boys' "Left to My Own Devices" with professional dancer Derek Hough. During the performance I could feel that we were moving in synch with each other and thought the audience was loving it. My hunch was confirmed when each judge offered the most kind praises. When the cameras showed *Mark's* reaction after the dance—his longevity on the show that season depended on my success—it was obvious that he was psyched about the performance we'd given. When the camera shifted to competitive Carlos, though—who'd gotten an amazing score of 39 out of 40 that week—I think he suspected I'd beaten him. Because he looked like someone was forcing him to clap. I know my baby.

For the first time in the competition, I was actually excited to hear what the judges' scores would be.

Carrie Ann Inaba? Ten!

Julianne Hough? Ten!

Guest judge Maksim Chmerkovskiy? Ten!

Bruno Tonioli? Ten!

Derek and I had earned the first perfect score of the season!

As Mark and I were figuring out what dance to do for the ninth episode, I felt led to tell him about the origin of my struggles with food. "I remember," I shared, "I was shooting this movie, and the producers just kept telling me, 'You're too fat.'"

I explained how, from that moment, I had an eating disorder for the next seven years of my life. I shared how the insecurities I'd felt about my body stemmed from that experience. When Mark heard this, it shaped the contemporary dance we'd perform that week. I'd be playing myself, he explained, and the character he'd represent would be the bulimia. It's a wild dance where he attacks me and scoops me off my feet. I try to resist, struggling to get away, and yet often ending up back into his grabby arms. At the very end of the powerful dance, I wrestle loose and walk away to freedom. That week's dance came easily to me, as easy as salsa, perhaps because I was so invested.

The experience of sharing that story publicly was powerful for me, personally, because it was the part of me that I'd always hidden, fearful for anyone to find out.

In fact, I remember that when I'd been eighteen years old, actress Katharine McPhee had appeared on the cover of *People* magazine, revealing that she'd suffered from bulimia. And at that time my mom remarked to me, "See, she came out, and now people will forever see her only as having bulimia. They'll never be able to see her any other way." Her message was clear, and I started believing that if anybody ever found out about my eating disorder, it would be the death of me. I now know that my mom said it thinking she was being *protective* of me, but it really stuck with me in a harmful way.

And yet as I got healthier, I knew I wanted to share my story because I wanted to help people. That moment had come. Sometimes those of us who are tangled up in disordered eating believe that talking about it will somehow keep it alive. That's a lie. The opposite is actually more true: when we refuse to acknowledge and expose our eating disorder, it continues to live inside us; when we expose it to the light, by speaking honestly, it no longer controls us because it thrives on secret darkness.

At the end of that evening's show, both Carlos and I found ourselves sharing the hot seat. After other contestants were announced "safe," we were the two remaining celebrity dancers being considered for elimination, and one of us would have to go home. (As much as I hated the position we were in, I have to admit that that's good TV, right there.) Mark and I stood side by side with Witney and Los, knowing that one pair would be eliminated and one would remain.

I want to tell you what it's like to stand on that spot, in front of those cameras, and the eyes of millions. You know it's television, you know it's a show, but the emotions you're feeling and the threat of being ejected are so real. You know it's produced and dramatized, but when you're in that moment, you feel like this is the biggest competition in the world—more monumental than warring nations, more critical survival than the Hunger Games. You're overwhelmed with feels. You're exhausted from the rehearsals, you're tired from the emotions, and you are standing on that platform with the world awaiting your fate. Audience members in the studio and at home are holding their breath. The most dramatic music is slowly building to heighten the tension.

As that music pulsed in the background, Tom Bergeron announced plainly, "Alexa and Mark, and Carlos and Witney, this ninth week of competition, the couple leaving right now is . . ."

I swear that the pause between those words and Tom naming which one of us would go home felt like *three hours*. Finally, he spit it out.

"Alexa and Mark."

If you watch Carlos's face when it was announced, you see him cringe with pain before turning to embrace me. "I wanted it to be me," he commiserated. Soon he was bawling. (I thought it was sweet, but today he's embarrassed by it.)

What felt super crazy-making that night was that I'd received another round of perfect 10s from the judges! Yet I was eliminated from the competition because the scores were a combination of both viewers' votes and judges' scores over two weeks. So not even my perfect score saved me from elimination.

Boy, it was rough.

When interviewed after the blow, I offered, "I'm so happy we ended on this note. If we're gonna go out, this is how I want to go out."

I meant it.

The way the show works is that when you're booted off the island, they put you on a flight to New York, and the next morning you're being interviewed on *Good Morning America* and *The View*. It's rough, but it's in the contract along with other fine print. So you're exhausted, you've had no sleep, and you've gotta smile. (Welcome to our world.)

While Carlos should have been in rehearsals with Witney on Tuesday, he hopped on the plane with me that night. Because Mark and I had tickets in first class, and Los was stuck with a window in coach, we asked the person beside him, in the middle seat, if they wanted to sit in first class. Problem solved! I was so touched that he wanted to be with me in New York to give me his love and support. Not for the cameras, just for me. He gave up one of his rehearsal days, flew back after my day of press, and started prepping for the tenth week of the show.

Until that moment he'd been relatively levelheaded (for Los) about the possibility of going all the way and taking home the coveted Mirrorball trophy. We were there to have fun together and whatever happened, happened. We agreed we'd support each other throughout the competition, and if we both made it to the finals, that's when we'd battle it out. Los *really* wanted us to make it to the end together. And once I was eliminated, he went a little nuts. Feeling like his girl had been robbed, he got crazy competitive about winning and returned to the show to dance with a vengeance. Truly, he was like some macho dude defending the honor of his lady. My man's got fire.

The next week—same week as the rehearsal he missed—he got all 9s and 10s from the judges. Boom! And when he reached the finals, he finally earned his perfect score: all 10s in both the foxtrot and freestyle dances. But because TV is TV, Carlos was eliminated from the competition on night one of the finals. It's no surprise that I think they missed the mark on that one, 'cause that boy can *dance*. But the adorable Bindi Irwin took home the Mirrorball, and we couldn't have been happier for her. She is one of the kindest young adults we have ever met. Her mother, Terri—*equally amazing*—raised her and her brother, Robert, to be kids with pure, genuine kindness.

While either one of us winning the Mirrorball would have been awesome, when we packed up our lives and left the show, we'd done what we'd come to do: we had so much fun dancing; we supported each other as husband and wife; we shared the most important, vulnerable parts of our personal stories with the world. In that respect, we'd done what we believed mattered most.

And at that moment, being honest about our struggles and sharing our journey with Christ were the most important things in our lives. But a new little thing was about to change our lives forever.

CHAPTER 9

BECOMING A DAD

LOS

Baby, I gotta pee," Lex announced as we pulled in the driveway, hopping out of the car and dashing inside.

"Yeah," I said to the spot where she'd been. "You go, babe. I've got the bags!"

It had been a couple of weeks since we'd returned from an incredible twelve-night cruise to the southern Caribbean. We had just driven over an hour from a meeting, so it made sense why Lex had to pee so badly. I was getting the car settled in the garage when my beloved stumbled out the front door. Wide-eyed, she looked a little dazed and was holding something like a popsicle stick in her hand.

"Babe," I asked, "are you okay?"

The zombie look on her face was freakin' me out a little bit.

Holding up the stick, she announced, "I'm pregnant."

Suddenly my eyes grew as wide as hers. And in seconds we were jumping up and down and shouting. "We're having a kid! We're having a kid!" we both yelled in unison.

"How did this happen?" she screamed.

"It was the boat!" I yelled. "It was the ship!"

In the wake of a huge storm damaging a Royal Caribbean cruise, travelers were hesitant to book trips. So the company contacted us to invite us on a free cruise on *Anthem of the Seas*. All we needed to do was post on social media to remind people how safe it was to go on a cruise. When the request came, Lex and I didn't even need to discuss it. We were in. Only catch was that we had to leave immediately on a red-eye since the ship was departing from NYC the next day. So we quickly packed and made our cross-country journey. Though it went by too fast, the cruise was incredible. And before we knew it, we were in the car driving back home. Little did we know, we'd *somehow* made a baby. (Was I completely on board for the baby-making process? Always.)

Nah, I'm not gonna pretend like I don't know how it happened. Lex was tracking her ovulation and temperature and all that lady stuff, and she *told* me when it was time. If Ocean was conceived when our math says he was conceived, I'd just gotten to the gym when she texted me a smiley face, signaling it was go time.

During the first few years of marriage, we'd prayed about having a child and felt like God was leading us in that direction. During the previous six months when we'd been trying to conceive, every month we weren't pregnant was a disappointment. Lex would pee on a stick, read the negative result, and keep her chin up.

We'd tried for several months, and with concern in her voice, Lex had asked me, "Did I mess up so bad that I won't be able to have a baby?" She worried that the damage she'd done to her body as a result of her eating disorder would prevent her from being able to become a mom.

"No, babe," I assured her. "It's gonna happen. God's gonna make it happen."

Though I knew she harbored this concern in her heart, I witnessed her signature confidence in God's provision throughout that season. As we waited on God's timing, she knew that He had her. Had us.

We'd been married just over two years when we found out we were expecting, and we were over the moon with excitement. It felt like the right next step. I can't explain it any other way. It just felt right. We kept the good news as our secret for a few months, and when we decided to start sharing, we had a blast.

When Lex's sister Makenzie visited our home, Lex handed her the string of black and white ultrasound pictures of our little nugget in utero. Makenzie just started bawling with joy.

It was also super fun to tell our dads. Lex's stepdad, Eric, was thrilled for us. We were visiting Florida when we got to tell my dad, who was becoming Papa Pena. He'd always loved Lex, but when he found out she was carrying his first Pena grandchild, he just wouldn't stop hugging her. But I think her dad's reaction was my favorite. We told him together in our kitchen, and after he found out he said to me, "I used to like you, but now I *love* you." (Good to know.)

For some reason we were convinced we were having a girl. And, honestly, I really got attached to that imaginary little baby girl. We even named that little peanut Hero. But after our twenty-week ultrasound, we couldn't wait any longer. Lex's main doctor was out of town, so we drove to a small ultrasound studio somewhere in Glendale.

The woman was Russian. Strong accent. We were the only people there, so she took us in right away. She looked at the screen and let us know that the tiny being we thought was our daughter was really our son! Her actual words were "Oh, there it is."

I responded like any person would. "There is what?"

"Right there," she added. Lex and I shared a look. I was supposed to believe that this blurry, pixelated part on the screen was a penis? (Sorry, I'll only say that word this once.) Not that we were disappointed, but for months we had been talking and making videos with our baby girl in her mommy's belly. While it did take me a minute to say goodbye to Hero, I quickly got on board with this boy we planned to name Ocean, who was about to turn our lives upside down.

Not to brag, but my woman *won* at pregnancy. She learned everything there was to know. She ate healthy. She exercised. She even filmed the Hallmark movie *Ms. Matched* during her first trimester. She was a beast. I mean, she was so ready that whoever was inside her was probably just gonna pop out when she hit the magic forty-week mark.

Except, it wasn't like that at all.

When Lex was having contractions at the end of November—on her actual full-term *due date*!—we totally thought it was time to have that baby.

Nope. Not time.

On the morning of November 29, we were super sure that baby was on his way out. Lex was really feeling those contractions again at two in the morning. So I offered her every comfort

I could think of. Both of us were shocked that nine days later we were still waiting to see our baby.

But then on December 6 at midnight, the contractions started again. This time our baby was definitely coming.

Or so we thought.

I brought Lex popsicles, and I put her in a hot bath. I played one of my favorite Christmas movies, *Christmas with the Kranks*, and started timing her contractions. I mean, I thought it was the perfect atmosphere for a wife trying to squeeze a human out of her body.

Her contractions were steady, but she jumped back in bed to rest.

Wait? I thought we were having a baby tonight?

An exhausted Lex slept in intervals of four minutes. Poor girl. But she was tough. My girl was tough!

Around two the next afternoon we made our way to her doctor's office where they put her on this noisy machine that would measure her contractions. I felt helpless not being able to do anything to make it better, so I asked, "Should I go to Whole Foods?" It's one of her favorite places.

She ignored me, because she was *focused*.

After Lex was examined, they told us she was dilated only one centimeter. If you don't know the dilation math, the baby's not coming through the tunnel until the woman's cervix is dilated to *ten* centimeters. So they sent us home to hang. Dutiful, we went home.

By nine that evening she was having crazy contractions that were just two minutes apart. More baby math: you're supposed to go to the hospital when they're *three* minutes apart, long before they ramp up to being *two* minutes apart. We quickly jumped in the car, but not before I could lay a towel down on the passenger seat. *Hey, don't judge me!* I did not want her water to break all over my car. (I'm still working on myself.)

On the forty-minute trip to the hospital, praying and breathing through the pain, my angel playfully quipped, "Whoops, my bad. We should have left sooner."

In the hospital at two in the morning, she was having more crazy contractions and had moved down to the floor to her hands and knees. Whatever works. This is when our all-natural birth plan changed. All that means is that the pain was so brutal, Lex opted to have an epidural, which could numb the pain some. Mad respect.

The next morning, when Lex was only dilated four centimeters, Dr. Crane decided to break her water, which is the sac of fluid in her uterus surrounding the baby. At least it didn't break in my car! Okay, so more baby math: once a woman's water breaks, the body is supposed to pick up the pace, for the baby's safety, and squeeze that baby out within twenty-four hours. That's the big idea. So the clock was now ticking.

Six hours later, when Lex was only dilated to five centimeters, she mused, "I must be a comfy room for him, because he's not wanting to come out at all." She wasn't wrong.

Then this crazy woman started singing a BTR song, "Oh, we're halfway there . . ." Even in the midst of all the pain, she was still a goofball. That's my Lex.

If a woman hasn't delivered twenty-four hours after her water breaks, it's time for doctors to perform a Caesarean section, cutting her open and taking the baby to protect it. (Sorry, I had to get graphic about it.) While Lex totally would have signed on if that was necessary to keep our baby safe, she was really, *really* hoping to deliver vaginally, so that instead of getting stitched up immediately after delivery, she could be holding our son to her chest and bonding with him.

At nine that night, twelve hours after Lex's water had been broken, a nurse came in and turned off the epidural that had been keeping her more comfortable.

"You sure you want to do that?" Lex asked.

When a woman is able to feel again—feel pain, feel her parts—she can be a more active participant in the pushing process. And it was time to push!

Gosh, I felt so helpless as the love of my life labored mightily. I held her hand. I stroked her hair. I kissed her forehead and told her how amazing she was doing. When she pulled me close, I knew we were having a special moment.

"Please stop talking," she said as she clenched her teeth through a contraction.

I smiled and gave her some space. There was nothing I could do to make the incredible, amazing work she was doing any easier. She was truly a birthing rock star.

At 10:04 p.m., Mr. Ocean King PenaVega squeaked out his first cry and drew his first breath. As my son's squishy face was pressed against his mother's chest, I was bawling. I mean bawling like . . . well . . . like a baby. To this day Lex will tell you that holding that "warm goopy thing" (her words) was the most incredible feeling ever. She still gets a little melty just thinking about it.

Throughout that first night—but really, what day was it anyway?—Lex fed li'l Ocean faithfully every three hours. She was a champ. I was overwhelmed.

I remember at one point saying to Lex, "What did we do?"

Our lives had changed forever, and I was kinda having second thoughts. Maybe I was just tired and annoyed from all the crying (I had a lot of growing up to do). And the next morning, after what felt like a lifetime with no sleep, we got to take our boy *home*, where Papa Pena was waiting to welcome us.

We spent a lot of Ocean's first year in an apartment in Vancouver where I was working on the CW show *Life Sentence*. Honestly, it was a rough year. We were living in cold and rainy Canada while we were working a new job and adjusting to a new baby in new surroundings. Lex and I both agree this was the toughest time in our marriage, and we were so glad when it ended—and that we'd survived.

But becoming a parent has been one of the most fulfilling roles we've ever had. It has taught Lex and me more about God than we could have imagined. For example, when our kids are learning to walk, and they stumble and fall, we rush to pick them up. We naturally want the best for them. When they're really trying to figure something out—whether it's tumbling or a puzzle or reading a word—we want nothing more than to help them figure it out. When they're wrestling to choose between right and wrong, we want to help them see the right path forward. And when they choose to do wrong? When they choose to sin? When they mess up? Yeah, it's frustrating. And we let them know, plainly, that it's wrong. But we never stop loving them with our whole hearts. And when they turn to us and say, "I'm sorry, that was wrong," we are eager to answer, "Forgiven. Now that you know that, let's move forward." Because of our kids we get these glimpses into God's heart for Los and Lex.

When I met Lex, she was this fascinating, vibrant single girl. We were both growing in our faith, I loved spending time with her, and I knew I wanted to spend the rest of our lives together.

Then I had the privilege of knowing her as my wife. In marriage she is, in a lot of ways, our family's spiritual compass. When I get an idea—"Hey, babe, let's buy a catamaran and spend three months every year sailing"—I am ready to go. I've done the research, I've shifted the finances, and I'm packing the sunscreen. Lex, though? She *listens* to God. Proverbs 16:9 says, "In their hearts humans plan their course, but the LORD establishes their steps." In our relationship I'm the first part of that verse, and she's the second. Lex always wants to see what God is going to say about our plans, and I treasure that about her. And together we've learned the hard way that if God's not in it, we don't want to be either. Whether it's a house we want to buy, a job we want to take, or a child we want to make, we've discovered that when we bull-headedly push ahead—and by *we*, I of course mean *me*—without God's leading, we regret it. And because Lex does seem to have this direct line to the Almighty (my words, not hers), I know that if she's hesitant, I don't want to move forward. It has become so important to us to be on the same page with our goals and dreams.

When Lex and I look around at our peer group, a lot of our friends haven't been interested in getting married and having kids. And in a lot of ways, I get it. When you're single, you do what you want to do, when you want to do it, and how you want to do it. I'm not throwin' shade—when I was single, for those brief moments, my life looked like that too. But when you marry, you essentially have to give up something so that your marriage can thrive. On our wedding day, when Bishop held the wedding rings Lex and I exchanged at our private ceremony, he *told us* that this is how marriage works. There *are* sacrifices to be made. He noted the circular design of the rings, describing how they were solid and there was no break in the circle. And he compared that unending circle to Lex and me. Now that we were becoming *one*, we needed to make sure that our marriage stayed as strong as our rings, adjusting as we go to make sure that we keep our circle whole. Since that day in late 2013, we've learned that marriage is about give and take. Believe me when I say that what we've received in marriage has been worth anything we've had to give up. I think it's fair to say that Lex has given up way more than I have.

Before we married, everything she'd known was acting. If she was on set, she was in her happy place. If she was off set, she was dreaming of being back on set. It's where she came alive. But once we married, we realized we needed to figure out what our work- and home-life balance would look like. And once we started having kids, there was even more to balance! For eight months when Ocean was an infant, Lex paused her own acting career and cared for him in that Vancouver apartment while I worked on a show. That was a rough season for me, but I know it was even harder for her.

I don't take it for granted that in many ways Lex has chosen to put her deep passion for acting on hold in this season in order to honor the life we're building together. It doesn't mean she doesn't work, but it does mean that she's prioritizing our family.

(And, to be fair, I can't nurse these babies.) Even agreeing to leave Los Angeles and move to Maui was, for Lex, a sacrifice she made for our family. We both know she'll continue to perform, but in this season she's shifted her priorities to focus on the family we're growing. And when the time is right, we'll make space for her to take the right job, write the next book, and do all the things God has called and gifted her to do. Honestly, I see that as an important part of my mission as her husband: *How do I support her so that she can be the woman she was made to be, both personally and professionally? What do I need to give up so that she can thrive?*

I want to see Lex thrive because she is the root to our tree. She's so devoted to us that sometimes she forgets that she needs water too! So I give her water. Truly, her faith and conviction help me walk in the narrow way. Her faith makes me want to seek God more.

When Kingston was an infant, Lex was offered a Hallmark movie called *Taking a Shot at Love*. Was I sure that I could manage two kids if I sent her off to shoot for six weeks? I wasn't. We were also in the middle of a move from our first home on Maui to our second. It was terrible timing, but I knew she really needed to be back on set doing what she loved. Together we decided that we'd find a way to make it work. Six weeks and one broken leg (Ocean's) later, she came home. We'd survived!

We've committed ourselves to seeking God's plan for our marriage and our family, and day by day, year by year, God is guiding us into the future He has for us.

Lex and I are a strong team when it comes to parenting. We balance each other out. She's naturally comforting and is learning when she needs to enforce the rules. I'm the natural enforcer, and am learning—from Lex—how to comfort our kids.

A lot of what I naturally bring to parenting is what I experienced when I was growing up. So when I'm at the grocery store or airport and I hear kids sassing their parents, talking back, doing whatever they want, I'm kind of blown away. That would *never* have flown at my house when I was a kid! I grew up with a healthy fear of my parents. I understood what they expected of me, and I knew that if I let them down, there would be consequences.

One day when I was in middle school, I was arguing with my parents about doing homework when my friend Jeff got to play outside. They had already spoken their piece, and they weren't budging.

"But Jeff gets to—" I began to whine.

My mom snapped, "Well Jeff isn't our child. You've got us for parents."

Frustrated, and out of arguments, I snapped. Even as the words were coming out of my mouth, I knew they were gonna get me in trouble. "I'd rather be in *jail* than live here!"

That, it turns out, was easy enough to arrange. When I came home from school the next day, I walked to my room, but something was off. I opened the door and my room was empty. Did I go to the right house? Every poster on my wall had been removed. Every sports pennant was gone; my hockey sticks, my favorite kicks, were missing. My desk, my chair, and my dresser were gone. In the middle of the room was a mattress, and when I opened my closet, I found only a few school clothes still hanging inside.

Shocked, I stumbled back out to the kitchen. My mom was waiting for me, sitting coolly at the kitchen table.

"You said you'd rather be in jail."

I hadn't even thought about my vain threat from the night before.

"Well," she said, "welcome to jail."

I was speechless.

"It was a joke. C'mon! I was kidding!" I pleaded.

For the next two weeks, I'd come home from school and go to my jail cell. I was allowed to eat dinner with the family, and then I was sent back to jail. If I got thirsty in the evening, my mom would bring water to my door.

Most of my friends thought my parents were crazy strict. And they weren't wrong. But I actually think that having those clearly established boundaries helped me learn to respect authority.

Our kids aren't yet to the age where they're tempted to push the limits too far with us. I mean, they sometimes say no to us, but a quick time out and they are back in order. But if they're like every other kid on the planet, we know that day of pushing limits is coming. And that's why we communicate to them now that we expect them to respect our judgment. Respect our decisions. Respect our rules.

If one of my kids tells me he'd rather be in a prison than live in my home? You bet your butt I'm going to put a little mattress on his floor and bellow, "Welcome home, señor!"

Lex shared that when she was growing up, she was a people pleaser and a rule follower. Basically, she was a parent's dream child. But her mom ran a tight ship. She wanted to know everything her kids were up to. So there were cameras keeping watch throughout the house, and Lex didn't even have a door on her room (like jail)! In an adolescent fit, and her last effort in the fight for her privacy, she threatened her mom, "If you don't give me a door, I'm going to start masturbating and everyone will see!"

She got her door.

Like a lot of young parents, Lex and I are picking and choosing what we replicate from our experience as kids and what we want to do differently. And as we get to know each of our children, we're learning that parenting is not a one-size-fits-all endeavor.

Ocean has a strong personality, and we'll go head-to-head. He's got that fiery Latin blood. We've learned that his love languages are gifts and acts of kindness, just like me! And he's a performer. He loves to get on stage and be like, "Look at me! Listen to me!" (He may be a little tone deaf.) But even though he's like me in a lot of ways, he is definitely his own little man, and we continue to discover new things about him.

Kingston is different from Ocean in many ways. When I lay down the rules with Kingston, or even just ask him to stop what he's doing, my boy starts crying. He's sensitive, that one, and we're learning that we need to nurture him a little differently. His love language is words of affirmation, like his mama, so we remind him on the regular, "I love you. You're so smart, bud. You're so precious." And that boy has some musical gifts. He can follow any key. Almost. It won't surprise me if he gets into music, but we'll see what it is that will light his fire. Right now he gets excited just playing with bubbles outside!

And on top of managing our two boys' completely different personalities, we're in the process now of learning who our daughter, Rio, is going to become. It is so fun to see her growing and changing every day. (I predict she's gonna be a daddy's girl.)

Right now my favorite thing to do with the boys is to play with them in the pool after dinner just as the sun is setting. It's a win for everyone, because it gets a lot of their energy out right before bed. Because they know that I'll toss them in the air, as soon as Kingston learned to put a few words together, he began to ask after each dinner, "Daddy, pool?"

And when bedtime comes, we want these kids to know that we love them and God loves them. Is it like herding cats? Yeah, it is. But these cats are so worth it.

After their teeth are brushed, the boys climb into bed. And I don't mean beds plural, I mean *bed*. Right now they're sleeping Willy-Wonka-grandparent style, foot-to-foot, under their shark bedsheets, in the same twin-size upper bunk bed. Sharing the same single fluffy blue blanket. (And it's as cute as it sounds.)

First, we'll have a story. I might make up a tale about what happened during their day and embellish it with some crazy touches. Every story ends with one of us saying "the end." Obviously. Otherwise, the story is clearly not over, and Ocean lets me know.

Then we sing a song. It's not a song you've ever heard before, but it's a PenaVega favorite. One day I started making up a song as Ocean was resisting sleep, and the lyrics were something along the lines of, "Ocean, go to sleep . . ." Ocean thought the song needed a jazzy little touch, and so he added "Bing Bong Bing." For those in the know, this is a random phrase from the animated show *Peppa Pig*. So this original song that's become a classic is now the nightly litany signaling that it's time to sleep. We sing it three times, and on the third go-around, we end on a high note and everyone tries to harmonize. It hasn't sounded great . . . yet. We're getting there.

Then we pray. The prayer begins as a prayer of protection over our family and friends. We name them all. *Each one.* And Ocean lets us know if we forgot someone. That kid is smart! Then we suit everyone up (not literally) in the same armor that finally helped Lex defeat her eating disorder: the belt of truth, the breastplate of righteousness, feet fitted with the readiness of the gospel, the shield of faith, the helmet of salvation, and the sword of the Spirit (Ephesians 6:14–17). Once we're armored up, we recite affirmations that were given to Lex and me by our friend and mentor, Ginger. If you don't have your own nightly routine, I welcome you to appropriate ours. It goes like this:

> *I'm special.*
> *I'm loved.*
> *I'm worthy.*
> *I'm not rejected.*
> *I do matter on this earth.*
> *I will do mighty things for Jesus.*
> *I am the righteousness of God.*

(For the record, you're welcome.)

By the end of the whole rigamarole, Lex and I are fast asleep and the boys stay up a few more hours to talk to each other about the day. (JK. Opposite.)

Can I brag a little on my amazing wife? I think we've established that she's the incredible wife who makes me better every day. But she is also the most incredible mother to our children—and actually not just ours. She is selfless. She puts the kids and me before herself. And she'll tell you that the order of her priorities is: God,

Carlos, and kids. (Sometimes I have to remind her to put herself on that list.) She's our rock. Daily I watch her serve everybody else around her without even thinking about what it is she wants and needs.

So part of my job is to help her get at that.

"Babe, what do you need?" I'll ask.

"Nothing," she'll chime, "I'm good."

"No, really," I'll push, "what is it that you need right now?"

"I'm fine," she'll assure me.

But I'm not about to let it go. I'll dig and dig and dig until I finally wear her down.

Weary, defenses battered, she'll sometimes admit, "I'm *so* tired."

And I've learned that "tired," for Lex, means that she needs more than physical rest. She needs time alone with God. She needs to reconnect to her passions. She needs room to pursue something separate from the kids and me.

Of course. So we try to get her what she needs the way she provides so much of what we all need.

Remember how when Lex dated her first love, Nick, as a teen, and he'd tell her he loved her, she'd answer, "Same here"? She wasn't used to saying "I love you too" because they weren't words that she'd heard often growing up. I didn't either. But from the moment she pantomimed "I love you!" to me on the 405 Freeway, I wanted to keep telling her I loved her for the rest of our lives. And today, we do. They are the three words in our home that our children hear us say to each other and also say to them.

Ocean is saying it a lot these days.

He'll just walk up and tell me, "I love you, Dad."

And then my heart melts.

As Kingston is just beginning to get some words under his belt, we'll tell him, "I love you," and wait for him to respond, "I love you!"

More often than not, though, he answers, "*Love me!*"

Which cracks us up. I have a feeling he's going to be my little instigator.

"No, bud," we'll coach, "you say '*I love you.*'"

Then, grinning, he'll take another stab at it and yell, "*Love me!*"

Done.

The thing that both Lex and I craved from our parents, the words we longed to receive, are the ones we're showering on our children.

We want our kids to know that we love them, and we also want—*more than anything*—for them to know that God loves them. We want to instill the love of Christ in them as they grow up. We're not happy for them to just know about Jesus, like He's only another character in one of their storybooks. When Lex and I were growing up, we both went to church and knew *about* God. And while Lex had a really soft heart that yearned to *know* God, knowing about God was where it ended for me. But we are praying that these little babies will come to know Jesus personally, and we're asking for God's help to teach us to be the parents we need to be for them.

As you might imagine, a week in the life of our family doesn't look like families where one or two parents commute to an office to work a Monday through Friday, nine-to-five job. (Though sometimes that sounds pretty good!) There aren't typical weeks, and we have no crystal ball to know where our family will be or what we'll be up to six months from now. But we are trusting God, and when opportunities come our way, we pray about them and try to make the best decision for our family.

In the last few years, Lex has been offered shows and movies where we'd need to move to someplace like Atlanta and all be stuck there while she shoots. And yet even when the money would be really good, we always weigh the opportunity against the costs for our family. (No offense, ATL.) And that means we've said no to some really great offers. We agreed not to chase the money—and at first that was hard for me. But because we value the beautiful family rhythm we have at home, in Maui, we're very careful about what we say yes to. And we keep our eyes open for those opportunities where we can work on projects together. Sure, there are moments where we have to be apart. But our priority is keeping team PenaVega together as much as possible. While none of our kids are in the biz yet and may never be, we're open to that possibility if it ends up being something that lights their fire.

Lex and I are loving this early season of parenting, and we look forward to seeing what comes next. What we know for sure is that family matters. And we know that, on a lot of days, work can wait.

When I think back to my life as a single dude, cruising around in my white Mercedes convertible with the license plate "WAZZZAA," I'm reminded that it was a *good* life. I had good work, I had fun toys, I loved hanging with my BTR boys, and I was in some relationships with really great girls. But I can also see the way God has used, and continues to use, both marriage and parenting to mold me into the man He created me to be. I am *better* because of Lex, and I'm becoming better as I parent the little humans with whom we've been entrusted. For me, marriage and parenting has been this *gym* God has used to make me healthier and stronger as I seek to know Him, love Him, and serve Him. And I plan to keep up this workout for a very long time.

CHAPTER 10

BECOMING A MOM

LEX

Yep. Los and I are different. And I want to *underscore* that. He's got that fiery hot Latin personality—and temper!—and I'm more chill. He'd tell you that he had an anger in him and that all of his dating relationships before me included this verbal sparring that eventually led to yelling. (He'd also tell you that it was *exhausting*.) But when we were dating I firmly announced, "I don't do yelling." And guess what? Out of his love for me, he has always honored that request-slash-announcement.

Carlos wants to hurry and go, while I'd rather take my time.

He hustles to make sure we're financially solid and we've got food in the fridge, while I'm content trusting that God will provide for us.

He's an extroverted introvert, which means he's often horrified by the thought of a party. This surprises a lot of folks, since he's so good with people. He *resists* the party, but then comes alive because he's such a dynamic people person. It's like that Bible study that met at our home the first year we were married: initially, he didn't want to have people all up in our home. But once it happened, he loved hosting friends and guests. I, however, *come across* as an introvert, but then actually do legit love parties, gatherings, and having people over. Go figure.

Like Los said, I love my work and find deep meaning in it. And while Carlos is great at the work he does on set, it's more like a hobby for him that pays the bills. He's grateful for the opportunities he's had and continues to have, but work just isn't what drives him.

Even our love languages are different. As he said, he's touched and blessed by acts of service. So he'd rather have me clean the house, or help him with his work, or wash the car than tell him the ten things I most love about him. Me, though? I am *all about* the words of affirmation. I don't care if he cleans ground-up Cheerios out of my car mats; I don't care if he buys me pricey gifts; I don't need him to give me daily backrubs. When Los tells me what he loves about me—as a person, as a wife, as a mom—my heart *melts*. I feel like it does something to me spiritually. I come to life! The gift I request every year for my birthday is for him to gather those words in a letter with at least seven thousand words. Kidding . . . but not. I *do* ask for a letter, but I can settle for fewer words. I know some girls want the diamonds and pearls, but I am all about the words. I've saved every card he's ever given me. It's not a tall pile, but it means the world to me.

So yeah, we're pretty different. But we've come to believe that our differences aren't accidental. Where Los is weak, I can help him. And when I need support, he's there for me. When he's stuck, I can offer him a fresh perspective, and vice versa. We've come to believe that we're better together, and that's the goodness God intends for marriage.

I mentioned that when I was growing up, my mom was pretty intentional about keeping us all together. So when I was on set, my sisters were dragged along. Because I saw other families split up because of the business, I value that my mom was committed to our being together. Today we mirror that example when either Carlos or I am working away from home—in Vancouver, or Atlanta, or New York; we also make every effort we can to stay together.

Not too long ago the boys and I were staying in Vancouver with Carlos when the poop really hit the fan. Carlos and I had been on set filming *Picture Perfect Mysteries* for Hallmark, and the boys had been really out of sorts. Most days, we'd start before the sun was up, and every break we got we'd race back to the trailer for me to breastfeed Kingston and Los to love on Ocean. Then I would race back to set and say a bunch of lines! All day. Each of the boys had had a major meltdown, and even though I was exhausted, I'd begged God to help me be the mom they needed. If you haven't experienced toddler "meltdown," just know that it can be a force of nature more powerful than any galactic foe you've seen in any Marvel movie, ever. When parents are nourished, and resourced, and grounded, we can help our kids navigate their big feelings. But when we're depleted, and exhausted, and empty? It can feel pretty brutal.

After one particular sixteen-hour day, we were finally back in the apartment, and I was frantically trying to cook dinner. Carlos took one look at me and saw how overwhelmed I was, and he just *got it*. It didn't take a rocket scientist to figure it out, since at that moment both boys were falling to pieces and I was on the verge of coming undone. The television was blaring, the soup on the stove was boiling, and the boys were wailing. Beelining toward the spot where I stood in the kitchen, Carlos grabbed me and embraced me with those strong arms. I mean, we were face-to-face, heart to heart, and without saying a word, he held me for two solid minutes. Ocean was screaming for a cookie, and when he started climbing the pantry to get it for himself, a box of angel hair pasta fell off a shelf and scattered on the granite floor. When Los loosened his hold, we both just started crying and laughing at the chaos and absurdity of the moment.

I don't know how he could have assessed the situation in the blink of an eye, but that man's strong embrace was exactly what I needed. As were the laughter and tears. It is actually one of my favorite moments we have ever shared together. Funny how what could have seemed like one of the hardest or worst days as a working mom turned out to be one of the best moments in our marriage, where I felt so seen. I am so grateful to God that I have been given Carlos PenaVega as a teammate in this crazy journey of marriage and parenting.

But even though I never could have imagined the life I'm living today, I wouldn't trade it for the world. On most days my attention is split between nursing a baby, getting kids dressed, preparing food for the older ones, helping them learn and grow, supervising play and exercise, and doing one thousand other things. If Carlos is home, he's helping me juggle all those balls.

But there are these moments when I'll sense that one child needs the kind of focused attention that just isn't possible to offer all day long. For instance, after Rio was born, Kingston was particularly emotionally needy, like a lot of kids who are being displaced as the youngest. And moment by moment, the fussing and feigned helplessness and neediness felt exhausting. But we realized that he was adjusting to not being the baby in the family anymore. And when we recognized that, we were better able to help him with his big feelings.

Handing Rio off to Los, I'd get down eye-to-eye with Kingston and ask him, "Are you my baby too?"

Then he'd flash that grin that makes my heart melt. And I'd hold him. And love on him. And give him every ounce of attention to remind him that he is worthy and precious and loved.

Or I might notice that Ocean is having really big feels as he's building a block tower one day with these soft fabric blocks. And when I pay attention and ask God to help me see what's going on, I realize that the fan has been blowing his blocks over and he feels overwhelmed. On top of this, he likes and needs things to be orderly, so when there's too much stimuli, his brain gets overwhelmed. God has helped us to notice those triggers and to help him recover.

"Hey, bud," I might invite him. "Let's turn off the fan, and turn down the music, and see if that helps."

I think that allowing us to see what's triggering our kids is one of the ways God helps us moment by moment. As parents, it's our responsibility to help our kids notice their emotions and find solutions when they're stuck. So we get down on our hands and knees, we comfort them, we help them discover a better way.

Here's the thing: I believe that God helps me navigate the stuff of my life every single day. And He can help you too.

When we first moved to Maui, the stresses of figuring out work and marriage and parenting an infant were taking their toll on us. I was convinced that God *could* help us, help me, but sometimes at the end of the day I'd notice that I hadn't *accessed* that help.

So I set this timer to *gong* every twenty minutes.

"Every time I hear it, God," I promised, "I'm going to talk to you."

So I trained myself to turn my eyes, and heart, and mind, and voice to God. If you've not done this before, I highly recommend it. Because, of course, as we're managing the stuff of our everyday lives—whether that's caregiving, or working in an office, or working at home, or anything else—we need those reminders.

Gong!

"Okay, hey, Lord," I'd begin, "this is a pretty ugly tantrum, but I know you're here with me helping me to love this child."

Gong!

"Just opened this huge, unexpected bill, so I'm trusting you to help us."

Gong!

"Seriously? The washing machine isn't starting right now? All our clothes are dirty, and we have a flight first thing in the morning. Help me, Lord."

When I pause to take that breather, and to invite God into whatever is happening, He has been so faithful to show up and to give me wisdom about how to handle things.

If you think it sounds a little simplistic, then you get it! It *is* simple. And God is so happy to meet us in the moments of our days.

In this season, I happen to be parenting. Maybe you're hustling to finish your degree. Or you might be working a program to overcome your addiction. You might be working a job you don't love as you work toward getting the opportunity to do the thing you *do* love. Or you might be in a hard season, emotionally, with a parent or a spouse or a friend. Wherever you find yourself, today, I promise you that God is waiting for you to pause, notice Him, and talk to Him. I know this, because *He* is that parent who's eager to be with His kids.

When Ocean was about nine months old, and we were down on the floor playing with him, he was surrounded by his toys: plush blocks, squeaky squeeze toys, crinkly fabric books, and more. I just remember trying to catch his gaze. But as I looked at his face, I couldn't quite get his attention. He was too busy clutching those sweet pudgy little fingers around a rubber ring to even notice I existed. Because I wanted to see that gorgeous little smile, though, I kept my eyes focused on him. But he'd caught sight of this colorful patchwork ball within crawling distance and was wriggling after it. Honestly, I was dead to him.

And in that moment, I understood the heart of God in a new way. His gaze is *fixed* on me. His heart yearns for me to look up at Him and smile. And it's not that I don't love Him. It's not that I'm unwilling to tip my eyes toward His. I'm just *distracted*. By texts. By Instagram. By grocery lists. By dirty dishes. By alerts. By YouTube. My eyes are focused on a hundred other things while God waits patiently for me to turn toward Him.

Certain Ocean would have plenty of other time in the day to explore his toys, I began scooping them up. Tossing them into a basket, out of his eyesight, I dropped down to the floor again. While I may need another approach when Ocean is fifteen, on that day my strategy worked! When I started making silly faces at him, he began giggling. Boy, the sight and sound of that kid laughing just made my heart want to explode. I can't think of anything more wonderful.

That day, a new prayer was born in my heart: "God, *please* take away all my toys." Now, I know that's a risky prayer. I hear it. But because of what's at stake—my relationship with my Father—it's a brave prayer I've continued to pray. I always want to have a heart that delights in my Father's face, and if anything gets in the way of that, I'm willing—no, I'm eager—to release it.

For both Carlos and me, parenting our kids has caused us to reflect on our own childhoods. There is so much that I'm thankful for in mine. Every physical need I had was met. I'm grateful that my mom prayed with us and took us to church. I thank God for the amazing opportunities that came my way to do that thing I felt like I was made for. And I had these amazing little sisters who were my best friends.

But, of course, there were also things that I wish had been different. I was so hungry for my parents to see me and hear me, and for a variety of reasons that wasn't what I experienced. And while I've forgiven my mom for what she couldn't give me, that feeling—of being unseen and unheard—stuck with me. (Ironic, isn't it? Before I reached age thirteen I was seen and heard by millions, but that still didn't fill that hole that only a parent can fill.)

Just like every new parent purposes to do some things differently than their parents did, one of my biggest goals as a parent has been for my children to experience being seen and heard. And the other is that they come to see and hear the God who loves them.

Los and I both want our kids to know Jesus. And I want that knowing to be more robust than just hearing us say "Jesus" a lot.

I want them to grow up to be kingdom people, to be fighters for the kingdom. And I don't mean that has to be as a pastor or as someone else who does ministry professionally. No. Whatever job or career they end up in, I want them to be so in love with God that they become builders of God's kingdom.

We also want for them to value *family*. Los and I both value family and make it a priority in our lives. And we're learning that "family" can look a lot of different ways. So when I chatted with Jodie Berndt, who wrote the book *Praying the Scriptures for Your Life*, I was intrigued by her comments about *Spy Kids*.

"I watched *Spy Kids* with my kids," she explained, "and I wondered who wrote the film. I wondered if they were Christians."

Isn't that crazy? Her point was that the film demonstrates the value of family. And I treasured her observation because those people—the cast, the crew, the directors—really were my family when I was growing up. Yes, I had my mom and sisters and stepdad, but I also had this family without blood connections who were so precious to me.

But if you haven't experienced the kind of family who protects you and nurtures you—I know a lot of people who haven't—that doesn't mean that you can't get in on the goodness of the kind of family we're made for. Specifically, we can enjoy that kind of love in the body of Christ. Carlos and I can both testify that we have both been loved so well by many of our brothers and sisters in Christ. In a season that felt lonely, when we didn't have our families to lean on, we found a family within the body of Christ who restored our hearts when we needed it most.

CHAPTER 11

WHAT IF LOVE . . . ?

LEX AND LOS

If you were to catch a glimpse of us on-screen—while you're munching warm, buttery popcorn in the theater—or if you see a picture online of us glammed up on the red carpet for a movie premiere, it would be natural to assume that life has been pretty smooth sailing for both of us. And we get it. We've both been *beyond* blessed and had some amazing opportunities. Or if you peek at our fam on the Gram today, we know the PenaVega life can look pretty sweet. (So you're *welcome* for us not posting the dirty diaper pics.) In so many ways, our life together is exactly what we always wanted it to be.

But you also know, now, that we've faced some obstacles along the way that we wouldn't have chosen. There *are* things that we'd change about our earliest years. As adolescents, we both hungered for meaningful friendships. Alexa battled an eating disorder and went through a divorce she wishes could have been avoided. Carlos was getting high and searching for happiness in the stuff he could buy. You've seen the ways that we were both searching for peace, meaning, and purpose. We were hungry for life that really is life (1 Timothy 6:19), and we tried to fill the void with that which, ultimately, didn't satisfy. But together we found that life in the person of Jesus. And we committed to building a life together based on God's Word. This has given us both a purpose and the daily hope we always longed for. Together we've become convinced that following Jesus is what we were made for, and we believe it's what you were made for.

About the time in our lives that we were both captivated by Jesus, we also met each other. Some may say that's coincidence. Some might say it's fate. All we know is that God's plan for our lives happened to be the complete opposite of the plans we had in mind. And we are so thankful He intervened when He did. So we've traveled this road of discovering how to live out our faith in Jesus together. We've experienced some amazing mountain-top moments, and we've struggled to claw our way out of a few dark valleys. And after each struggle we've faced together, we've paused to ask ourselves a few questions:

"What can we learn from this situation?"

"What is God teaching us?"

"What is the point?"

And what we've noticed in these challenges is that—whether we've screwed up, or maybe we've been hurt by someone else, or perhaps we've made a bad decision—when we turn our faces toward God, He shows up.

Every.

Single.

Time.

When we turn toward God, and seek Him, He is reliably present to help us. He's reliably present to help *you*.

And so we continue to ask that question—after a financial disaster, or a broken relationship, or a lost opportunity—"What is the point?" And as we listen for God's answer, again and again we hear His quiet whisper saying, "*Love.*"

Being loved by God is the point.

Loving God with our lives is the point.

Loving the people He puts in our path is the point.

Sharing God's love with others is the point.

Love is the point.

The reason our lives look the way they do today is because of God's *love*.

Because love is the point, we're both committed to growing spiritually.

When we were first married and Lex would slip out of bed early in the morning to spend time praying to God, it made me (Los) *mad*! Yes, I was a believer, but I was a *baby* believer. At that time I wasn't yet mature enough to see things from God's perspective. Instead, I'd see Lex leaving me and just get grumpy about it, roll over, and go back to sleep.

During that time I (Lex) remember having this sense that God was calling me to push away everything that was distracting me and to just *be* with Him. It was when we were living in our leaky, broken-down home and I needed to get away from that stress.

Get away from work. And, yeah, even from my hubby. So I'd slip out of bed in the morning and go into the prayer room, close the door, and handle my business.

Once I was in there, I just had this conviction that I was not coming out of that room until I'd encountered God. I actually set up three chairs: one for the Father, one for Jesus, and one for the Holy Spirit. And I talked to each one of them! Had someone planted a hidden camera in that room, they would have seen me going from chair to chair, talking to these invisible beings who were so palpable to me.

And they showed up. It was like I was floating in a dimension other than West Hills, and I felt this tingly sensation throughout my body. I felt so overwhelmed by God's presence, and by the joy that it generated in my heart, that I didn't even feel like I was on earth anymore. I had tasted a sliver of heaven.

While we can't dwell in those heaven-moments every day, we think God gives them to us so that we can see and hear and taste and touch who He is. We're not saying that's the only way to experience God, but we do think that it's important to make room in our lives to encounter the God who is real and wants to know us and be known by us.

We're delighted to report that today Carlos *helps* Lex carve out time to be alone with God. (Though, let's be real, with these babies running around, no one's holing up alone for very long these days! And that's okay in this season!) Los not only doesn't need this kind of quiet time isolation, it actually *kills* him. He'd much rather be talking to God while he's fixing something around the house or working in the yard. Our relationships with God look different, but we're putting ourselves in that space and giving God the opportunity to heal us and restore us.

If your life is full, we get it. Ours are too. But we keep listening to and responding to God's voice that's calling us to be still with Him.

Because love is the point, we are both committed to growing emotionally.

I (Lex) can tell you that I've seen so much growth in Los since we first met. Back then, he could get crazy jealous over anything and everything. But that's not who he is today. Because of the confidence he has in Christ, our relationship is solid, and he's not that jealous guy anymore.

And I (Los) can tell you that I've seen Lex grow in ways that have also shifted our relationship for the best. When we were first dating, I saw her as this spicy, outspoken girl who said whatever she thought. But, somehow, in the course of our relationship and early marriage, the people-pleasing Alexa came back. And although that sounds harmless enough, it was death-dealing for her. It means she wasn't speaking up when she needed to. Even about silly little stuff.

For example, because she knows I don't like sushi, whenever we'd be deciding where we wanted to go out, she'd say, "Whatever you want. Let's just get something you like." She was so worried about keeping the peace—at work and at home, even with me— that she wasn't using the voice that God had given her. But today she's brave to speak boldly and honestly.

"I want sushi! We never get sushi!"

And guess what? Her speaking up is good for our marriage! Today she's willing to say what she wants, to me and to others, even if it means not everyone will always like her. (I do, though. I like her a lot.)

Because love is the point, we're listening together for God's guidance.

It's pretty cool to see the ways that God leads us together.

One morning, when Ocean was our only child, Lex was praying in the shower.

Backstory: when we'd been dating, we both imagined having *lots* of kids. But after Ocean was born, we'd both felt that two kids would be enough for us. Only one more kid, we agreed, and at that point, we would be satisfied and done. We were absolutely on the same page about stopping after two kids.

Remember that passage in Proverbs that says, "In their hearts humans plan their course, but the LORD establishes their steps" (Proverbs 16:9)? Even though we make plans, God is the one who ultimately decides. And that's exactly what I (Lex) experienced in the shower that day when God whispered to my heart, "You're going to have lots of kids."

"Umm, excuse me, Lord?" I protested, "We are tired."

What's so weird about it is that when I received that word from God, I had a *peace* about it. And that's no small thing. There's no reason in the world I should have blindly accepted that alarming announcement, but He gifted me with a peace that surpassed my understanding. And when I say I had peace, I mean that if God were to give us a school bus–load full of kids, I was down with that.

It made absolutely no rational sense.

But even though I was uncharacteristically peaceful about it, I had no idea how Los was going to receive the revelation I was preparing to give him as I toweled off and got dressed. Because when I say we were on the same page about having one or two kids, I mean that we weren't even talking about it or praying about it anymore because *we had decided.*

"Humans plan their course . . ."

After showering, I joined my boys in the kitchen, as Carlos was pouring some cereal on Ocean's high chair tray.

Gathering my courage, I said, "Babe, this is going to sound crazy—"

And before I could finish my sentence, Carlos cut me off, blurting out, "I think we're going to have a lot of kids."

I was blown away.

Is he a mind-reading wizard right now?

"Los," I exploded, "what made you say that?"

"I don't know," he answered, "I was just praying about it, and that's what I heard."

"*Me too!*" I bellowed.

We shared with each other about how God had given us the same word in prayer, at the same time, and we just marveled at how good God is.

Friend, this is who God is. This is what God does. He leads us when we turn our hearts toward Him.

Because love is the point, in our marriage we're making each other better.

When we first met, we were a little starry-eyed. We saw only what was attractive in the other person. That's what the beginning of lots of relationships are like, right? At the beginning we're looking for someone who accepts every part of us. Of course, that's natural.

But we both believe that for relationships to be strong and healthy, you want to be with someone who's going to *challenge* you. Who—with love—will call you out on your stuff. We've both grown so much in our marriage, and that is in large part because we are committed to helping the other become the best version of themselves that they can be. That means that we're committed to challenging each other to be better. It's not always easy, but daily we are calling each other to level up.

If you're married, invest in helping your partner become the best version of themselves.

And if you're single, we encourage you to find someone who will help you level up. You won't be sorry you did.

Because love is the point, we're working to keep our marriage healthy and strong.

Do we know what it's like to bust our butts all day caring for these children and feel like sleepy zombies once they're down in bed? Yeah, we do. And sometimes the very best we can do at the end of the day is to give each other a quick kiss, watch three minutes of Netflix, and zonk out.

But because we value our marriage, and want to keep it as healthy as possible, we also try our best to make it a priority. That means that when Alexa is exhausted, I (Los) will take all the kids so she can recover. Or if Lex sees that I need her full attention, we'll let the big kids watch an episode of *Big Time Rush* so that we can get time together. Before we ever had children, we made a commitment to prioritize each other, our marriage, for the sake of our family.

And we're also keeping it fun. Too often we've seen couples who truly enjoyed each other when they were dating lose the playfulness in their relationship and even become indifferent to each other. So we keep laughing. We keep wrestling, with the kids and with each other! We keep carving out special time to be together. (Yes, sometimes it's in the bedroom.) Last week we ended up chasing each other around the house, poking fun at each other, almost like kids! We're choosing to embrace that youthful version of ourselves that each of us met when we were dating. We have our ups and downs. Some days we are better at marriage than others, better at prioritizing and being intentional. And some days we suck at it. It's like when you're potty training your kid: he does so well for one week, and then has that little accident. Marriage can't be perfect bliss all the time. Don't let people fool you; everyone's got crap. And it stinks.

Because love is the point, we're choosing the rest God offers.

Lately, in the midst of the crazy, we're hearing God invite us to *rest*. And the good gift He has for us is the same good gift He has for you. We hear the gracious invitation in Jesus' words: "Come to me, all you who are weary and burdened, and I will give you rest" (Matthew 11:28).

While we *wish* that the rest God gives means we'd get a solid eight hours of sleep every night, that magical gift has not been promised. But God is so faithful to give us the rest we need when we answer His invitation to "come to me." There was a season when we were able to carve out a whole day to spend with God. (We have a very distant memory of this being a real thing.) Other times we might set the alarm an hour early to create the holy space to be with God. But you know what? We can't always offer that much, and God is *still* faithful to meet us. Don't let me make you think it's easy. I (Los) struggle more than you could imagine with this. It's not in me to sit still and rest in Him. I just want to go, go, go. So I have to be intentional. Basically, I have to force myself to stop. Breathe. Pray. Listen. And I'm still working on it.

Last week Lex had an important phone call, and for three minutes before the call she paused to turn down the music, silence her phone, shut her eyes, and just give God those three minutes.

We know it sounds corny, but after those three peaceful minutes, she actually felt recharged! It was like taking a refreshing bath, and she was ready for whatever came next. For us, *rest* means resting in God. Whether you imagine yourself in a soothing, warm, bubbly bathtub or immersed in a clear, cool lake on a hot day, you can find rest with God and in God.

Truly, Lex might be cooking dinner while Nerf bullets fly through the living room and finger paint is being smeared on the window of the patio door. And on those nights, there are no three soothing minutes to be found! So as she stands in front of the stove, she'll close her eyes, take a deep breath, and release the stress she's carrying. Fifteen seconds later she's back in the chaos of the moment, but she took that *moment* to rest in God.

We see that kind of moment-by-moment peace as the kind of peace that we see in Jesus. When the world around Him was chaotic, and needy people tugged on Him (*We feel you, Jesus*), and the voices bombarding Him were *loud*, Jesus embodied this peace that really does pass understanding.

God is inviting us into something so much better than either the hustle-for-more or the make-it-through-this-day life. And the way we access that "more," that life that really is life (John 10:10), is through rest. When we choose to stop, we agree with God and we receive the goodness He has for us. (Why can this be so hard? It seems so simple. Right?)

He is constantly inviting us into those restful moments. He woos us to come to Him. Eager to hear from us, He welcomes us into His loving arms. And even though God is patiently waiting, receiving that life-giving rest and peace does require *something* of us. Yes, it's a good gift God gives, but we also have to make room to receive it.

Friend, this rest business isn't *our* big idea. In fact it's knit into the very fabric of creation: "On the seventh day [God] rested from all his work" (Genesis 2:2). God rests and God invites us to rest as well. It's what we're designed to do. It's even one of the ten commandments: "Remember the Sabbath day by keeping it holy" (Exodus 20:8). Rest was God's big idea to bless us!

Hustle culture hisses to us that if we rest, we'll fall behind.

But the goodness God offers is actually that when we rest we are refreshed and restored to be who He made us to be. Do you crave that clarity? I know we do, and it truly only comes when we lean into Him, completely clearing our minds of all our earthly desires and feelings. One question we love to ask God is "What do *you* want me to do?"

Our friends Jeff and Alyssa Bethke are being intentional with their family just like we're purposing to be with ours. And they have a rhythm of putting their phones away from Friday night to Saturday night. Isn't that the most healthy and wonderfully life-giving choice? They have really inspired us over the years. Their example and *consistency* in their lives have made such an impact on us every day. We're not saying we're the perfect family, but we make a choice every day to find those resting moments. (Even if it is while we are escaping from the chaos and using the restroom. You parents out there know what we're talking about! Sometimes it's the only place you can be alone.)

Because love is the point, we aim to live with integrity.

We're purposing to be true to who we are every day. When we were on a cruise a few years ago, a sponsor approached me (Los) about posting a picture on social of Ocean and me eating a particular brand of ketchup. And the compensation to do this was going to be . . . *quite substantial*. (Whatever number you're thinking, quadruple it. No, *octuple* it!) But here's the thing: I am just not a ketchup guy. So I'd be posting a picture presenting myself *loving* ketchup when, in fact, I don't love it at all. Did I consider for a second *becoming* a ketchup guy? Of course. But in the end I turned down the offer.

"Dude! You *passed*?" a friend demanded to know after I told him about the opportunity.

Yes.

Here's the thing: if I'm paid to act in front of a camera, I'm happy to do it. Cast me as the character who loves ketchup, and I'll convince every last viewer that I love ketchup. But what we're doing on social media, and what we're doing in this book, and what we're doing with people we meet is *sharing who we really are*. It's important to us that the people who know us and meet us and follow us can *trust* us. And the reason we want to maintain that integrity is because what we most hope to communicate means so much more than ketchup. We don't want anyone to second-guess what we're sharing. We want to live with integrity because, when we share about our faith, we don't want anyone to have an excuse to write us off.

It's not just on social either. One of the most amazing opportunities I (Los) have been given to share about my faith was on *Dancing with the Stars*. And while we'll be the first people to tell you that reality shows like that are *very produced*, we don't want anyone wondering if my testimony was some weird product placement ad! When I'm Carlos PenaVega, I'm representing Jesus Christ. We got such a big response after *Dancing with the Stars* from fans who thanked us for sharing our faith boldly. We want to honor their trust. I had to let go of any fear of what people might think. But since that one Monday night on the show, when I dug deep and shared some of my darkest moments, I became free. Free to share my testimony with anyone and everyone. Free to be the Carlos PenaVega that God created me to be. I mean, I'd just said it in front of millions of strangers on national television. What could be harder than that?

For both of us, living with integrity means that we are living a lifestyle that's consistent with our values. That's why, in these pages, we've wanted you to see both the good times and the moments when we've struggled.

Because love is the point, we purpose to live with consistency.

Something that's really important to both of us is living a lifestyle that's consistent with what we say we believe. In fact, it's one of the things we find so attractive about Jesus! He practiced what He preached, and as we follow Him, we are purposing to do the same.

We both saw it first in our friend Andrew. It's like those memes: "Tell me you're a breastfeeding mom without telling me you're a breastfeeding mom." Andrew told us he was a follower of Jesus without telling us he was a follower of Jesus. For example, we *saw* his love for people. We *witnessed* his faithfulness to Jesus. We *watched* as he was wildly generous with others. We *noticed* the way he cared for those in need. Through our friend we tasted and saw that the Lord was good (Psalm 34:8), and now we've purposed to show others Jesus through the lives we're living. And it looks a hundred different ways.

Living consistently, for us, means that while we still enjoy a glass of wine, we don't drink to get drunk.

It means that we turn down gigs that could compromise our integrity.

It means that we are emotionally and sexually faithful to one another.

For Alexa, living consistently means that she eats—and serves—food that is nourishing.

For Carlos, it means that he doesn't cuss anymore. (And TBH, when Carlos came to know Jesus, it's not that he even had to *try* that hard not to cuss; he didn't *want* those ugly words falling out of his mouth anymore.) A friend of ours once told us a story about a car accident she was in. The car went off the side of the road and down a hill. As the car was tumbling down an embankment, the first thing that came out of her mouth was "Jesus, please save us." I (Los) always think about what I would say. I've stubbed my toe or had something fall on me and had to bite my tongue as a curse word has been on its way out of my mouth. But I want to get to the point in life that no matter what happens, my first reaction is: *Jesus*.

Pipe breaks: "Jesus, guide me."
Flight gets canceled: "Jesus, show me why."
Wallet is lost: "Jesus, help."

What would be the first word out of your mouth?

We align ourselves with the teaching of Jesus so that others might witness, in us, the consistent lifestyle that points to Him.

Because love is the point, we are serving others.

We aim to serve others because that's what we see Jesus doing throughout the pages of the New Testament.

I (Lex) love the way that Carlos serves others. He is truly the friend that everyone dreams of. If you are moving, he will pack and move the whole house for you. If something needs fixing, he will show up and fix it. It could be three in the morning and he wouldn't even hesitate. He wants to be there for people. If guys are here working on the roof, he's getting them something to drink. If the cafeteria at church needs to be transformed into a sanctuary, he'll be there at seven in the morning setting up chairs.

My husband loves to serve. Acts of service is his love language! And he pours out those acts for everyone. My husband cares so deeply. That can be hard at times, because not everyone loves like he loves. But he still shows up—whether he is receiving that deep love in return or not. *That* is what makes him special. It's easy to love those who love you. But Los would show up to help his enemy in hopes of being a light and planting a seed. To me, that is his superpower. A deep lover with a giant heart!

And I (Los) can't say enough about how Lex serves everyone around her. She literally puts everyone before herself! I'll come home from doing errands, and she's standing at the stove cooking dinner for those of us in the house who have teeth *while* she's nursing a baby. And not just our baby. She's pumped her breastmilk to share with families who need it too! If I wake up in the morning and say I'm not feeling well, she literally has tea and herbs in my body before I even get out of bed. She is the first one up and sometimes the last one to sleep. Should I keep going?

(I hope she reads this! Maybe I'll get some husband points?) Lex is literally a gift from God. I was a capable young man, but I was lost, and she was the compass who kept me on the correct path. Without her dedication to our marriage, I don't know where we'd be. She is a teacher to all, and her passion to serve is unlike anything I've ever witnessed. I am lucky to have her as my wife.

We serve others because it's what we see Jesus doing.

Because love is the point, we are careful with our words.

A while back we were reading the book *Faith and Confession* by Charles Capps, which taught us that the words we speak are powerful. In fact, we believe that we can speak life or death with our words. The two of us were playing around one morning, and Carlos must have said something that was a little out of bounds.

So Lex announced, "Your words are very powerful, Mr. PenaVega."

To this day, we repeat this line to each other—and usually laugh about it—to remind us that what we say *matters*.

We really believe that there's power in everything we say. In fact, Proverbs 18:21 says that the power of life and death is in the tongue! Our words hold spiritual weight, and the Enemy wants those words to hurt others rather than bless them. And that's why we want to be very intentional about the words we use when we speak to each other. When we speak to our kids. When we speak to strangers. We want our words to bless and benefit and prosper others rather than to harm them.

Because love is the point, we invest in relationships.

We value relationships because Jesus values relationships.

We treasure Andrew, whom we've appointed as godfather to all our kids. He has become our brother as much as any of our blood siblings.

Jon and Hannah Frendl are as close as family as well. At the beginning of our friendship, Jon and Hannah were yearning for children but feeling discouraged by so many negative pregnancy tests. They were sharing this with us at our house and Alexa, who had an extra test in the bathroom, suggested that Hannah take one.

"I don't have to pee," Hannah said.

Lex pushed, "I'll bet you could get one drop out." (These tests actually need more than a drop, but Lex was determined.)

Bullied into peeing on a stick, Hannah finally obliged. Five minutes later, she wandered out of the bathroom in a zombie daze and uttered, "I'm pregnant."

Along with Andrew, these are our ride-or-die friends. And if either of us needs to pick up the phone to get wisdom or insight on something, they're the ones we dial.

Friend, knowing and following Jesus was never meant to be a Lone Ranger sport. We need sisters and brothers in the body of Christ to help us walk the walk. And each of these three has been so instrumental in helping us know and follow Jesus. We treasure them.

And of course there are countless other people we value. We invest in building relationships with people because we're interested in people's hearts. Surface relationships that never go deeper than small talk? No, thank you. Not for us. But when we meet friends who are interested in building something solid? We're in.

Because love is the point, we're working at healing relationships that are broken.

Just like everyone else, we have relationships in our lives that have been broken and have been in need of repair.

We have a term in our home for those people who can be a little tricky to love, and that is EGR: *Extra Grace Required.* (Thank you, George, for teaching us that!) We're on the same page in believing that you don't have to *like* everyone, but as followers of Christ you *do* need to love them. With some people, it's easy. But we all have EGR relationships in our lives. (And we might even be someone else's EGR!)

I (Lex) used to be really frustrated when people would cut me off in traffic. But one day this happened when I was driving with our friend Ginger, who's this solid believer who has a great relationship with God.

"Why don't you pray for them?" Ginger asked.

Uhhh . . . it had never occurred to me! So now I do pray for these EGR drivers.

Relationships can even get tricky with those who are our closest people. At one time our relationship with Andrew was broken. After feelings had been hurt, we didn't reach out to him for a season, and he wasn't reaching out to us. We knew our friendship needed help, and so did he. And the God who mends hearts and mends relationships was so faithful to help all three of us rebuild.

As you know, family is super important to both of us. But the truth is that some of the relationships we have with family members have been strained. Because we know that God heals what is broken, we've prayed about those relationships for years and are so excited to be seeing the beginnings of restoration.

Over the last year or two, Carlos's brothers have, individually, reached out to reconnect with him. And it's been beautiful to see those relationships being strengthened. It's what we are hoping and praying for all the relationships in our lives that have been in need of mending, and we continue to believe that God can do more than we can ask or imagine.

Honestly, when it comes to restored family relationships, we come by our passion honestly. My (Lex) mother's parents, my Nana and Papa, split up when I was an itty-bitty little girl, and they were soon with other people—my Nana with DC, and Papa with Jill—both whom I love. Two years ago we lost both DC and Jill. And after those losses, Nana and Papa got back together like the previous thirty years hadn't even happened! And Nana's faith has become a source of strength for her these last few years, as well. We know that God is a restorer of broken relationships!

Because love is the point, we're invested in the local body of Christ.

When we moved to Maui, it took us a minute to find the congregation that was right for us.

The first week we moved to our current home, our mail was delivered to us by this charismatic Hawaiian guy named Dallas. And Dallas, who seemed to be overflowing with love and peace and joy, was eager for us to visit his church. He described to us a place and a people who were just on fire for God.

Honestly, it sounded a little intense.

And we're a little gun shy about some congregations because we've seen churches that are more about religion than they are about Jesus. And we had no idea what Dallas's church was about, but we knew enough to be cautious.

"You coming this week?" he asked me (Los).

"You know what," I hedged, "we're actually going to be in LA this week, but maybe soon."

"Sounds good!" Dallas said. "I hope to see you there!"

"Maybe!" I said with a smile.

That Sunday, in Cali, we got to be with Jon and Hannah and their baby girl, Bella. We'd just finished a delicious meal and had retired to the couches in the living room when the conversation got a little more serious.

"We've been praying about when to tell you," Jon began.

It sounded ominous.

"And," he continued, "our friend is a pastor at this church in Maui, and we think you guys are ready for it."

Ready? Why did we need to be ready?

"Cool," Lex chimed in, "what's it called?"

Hannah answered, "We don't know the name of the church, but we know the pastor. We'll find out and hook you up."

"That would be awesome," I confirmed, "because we really

want to get connected and just haven't found the place that feels right for us."

We were a little surprised that they hadn't already told us that they had a pastor friend in Maui, but we trusted that Jon and Hannah are dialed in to the leading of God's Spirit and that the timing of them sharing this with us was just right.

Eight days later, back on the island, we rolled up in the parking lot of God's House. As we pulled Ocean out of his car seat, we saw other churchgoers all dressed pretty casually, climbing out of their own minivans, sedans, and SUVs, and walking in to church. A lot of them greeted us and made us feel so welcome. The men and women and children, young and old, who filed past our Chrysler minivan were Hawaiian locals, and White people, and Asian people, and even Black people and Latino people (who are more rare on the island). And guess who we saw there! Dallas, our mailman! The church he had been inviting us to was the *same* church Jon and Hannah had recommended! The name of the congregation, "God's House," was fitting for this body of believers who actually looked like the people of God described in Revelation who will one day be worshiping Jesus together in heaven. People in that delicious array of cultures and ethnicities who'd gathered to worship did it all kinds of ways: standing and sitting, eyes open and eyes closed, hands raised and hands lowered, some mostly still and others dancing in the aisles.

As we entered the high school cafeteria where the church gathered, the praise and worship team were already fired up. Slipping into one of the back rows, we remained standing as we joined others in singing the songs that were being projected onto huge screens in the front. A number of people were raising their hands as they worshiped. As the band gathered momentum and volume, we noticed one man stepped out into the aisle and was jumping up and down. And one woman was running laps around the sanctuary like she was at the Olympic time trials. Several folks had flags that they waved fiercely at the front of the sanctuary. And we even noticed a few people who were notably silent. Eyes closed, they continued to worship God in their own way. Both of us were struck by the fact that this was a joyful banquet feast where there was room for *everyone*. We sensed God's presence and Spirit and began to find ways to be a part of the vibrant family of God.

We encourage you to seek God's wisdom to find a healthy church home where worshipers are loving God and loving each other.

Because love is the point, we're sharing our faith with others.

So many people we know are looking for satisfaction. And yet the houses, and the cars, and the hookups, and the partying never fully satisfy. So many of us have believed the lie that if we just get the next thing, or the next person, we'll finally be happy. Finally be at peace. Finally be satisfied. But we can tell you that that's a losing game.

All of us hunger for something that's real and solid. And because the two of us have tasted that satisfaction in Jesus, we can't *not* tell others about Him. So if you're ready to live a life of meaning and purpose, we hope and pray that you will encounter the love of Jesus for yourself.

Again and again as we've asked God, "What is the point?" we hear His quiet whisper consistently saying, "Love."

Being loved by God is the point.

Loving God with our lives is the point.

Loving the people He puts in our path is the point.

Sharing God's love with others is the point.

Love is the point.

ACKNOWLEDGMENTS

In a world full of uncertainty and confusion, God has put people in our lives to challenge our ideas and comfort our emotions. Our journey thus far has been nothing but a prime example of God's handiwork. Every year we look back at the seasons we went through and thank God for the people who were positioned in our lives to help us keep glorifying Him.

The Hashimotos and Cristes: when we met, it was as if we had been friends forever. You challenged us in our faith and marriage. The heartbreaking loss of Tavin was the turning point for our family in so many ways. His life will never be forgotten and the impact he made on the PenaVegas has left us forever changed.

One of my (Alexa) longest friends, Cassidy Unruh: you have been such a wonderful example for me to look up to. You are an amazing wife and mama and have glorified God in every season.

The Sisterhood: you challenge me (Alexa) and you lift me up, but most of all you help me stay grounded and rooted in Him. Thank you for being one of the biggest blessings I could have ever prayed for. Like so many things in my life, I didn't know I needed you, but now I hold on to you for dear life!

John Carrabino: I (Alexa) have known you since I was six years old. You are not only the best manager I could have ever asked for, you are my friend. You are my greatest cheerleader. The love and kindness you have given me over these years have been healing in so many ways. I absolutely adore you. Thank you for being in my corner.

Our siblings: we have stood through thick and thin, and we've come through stronger and closer than before. We love you. We're so excited to continue to grow together and to continue growing our families! So many new blessings!

Our parents: thank you for sacrificing so much for us. Because of you we get to live our dream life today and instill so many important values you taught us in our children.

The Frendls: Jon and Hannah, you taught us what living for Jesus in the most selfless way looks like. We have never before witnessed *giving* the way your family gives and loves on others—with time, things, finances, and more. You show up. Thank you for your friendship and for being friends we can look up to.

To Chelsea Aaron: you are not only a talented photographer, *you* are one of our favorite people. Thank you for this beautiful cover. You brought our book to life! We love you and your family so much. May this be just one of *many* adventures we all have together.

To Jenny Baumgartner: from day one you have been such an encouraging voice to our marriage, our walk, and our life! Thank you for believing in us and thank you for giving us an opportunity to share our testimonies with the world. We love you!

To Margot Starbuck: we would be a puddle of thoughts and feelings without you. Thank you for guiding our words and making us sound like brilliant writers! You were one therapy session after another throughout this process. Thank you for turning our brain dumps into a book we are proud of.

The entire team that made this book possible: Alex, Sara, Brigitta, Stephanie, and the rest of the Nelson Books squad. It takes a team, and we couldn't have asked for a better one!

Last but not least, our beautiful babies: Ocean, Kingston, and Rio. The joy you bring us is unlike anything we have ever experienced. You make us laugh, you make us love deeper than ever before, and you bring a fullness to our lives that we cannot describe. We love you times a million.

ABOUT THE AUTHORS

Carlos and Alexa PenaVega are parents to three adventurous children: Ocean, Kingston, and Rio. They live on Maui but travel often for work. Between the two of them, they act, sing, and have a family vlog on YouTube called *La Vida PenaVega*. They competed against one another on *Dancing with the Stars* in the same season and star in multiple Hallmark movies. Carlos is a part of a successful boy band, Big Time Rush, and continues to make music and tour with them around the world.